"Patricia Zurita Ona offers thoughtful guidance and straightforward tools to help parents remain present for their struggling teen while learning to ride the push and pull of their teen's emotional tides. However, this book is not just for parents with troubled teens. Every parent will find something useful in this book, for what parent and what teen has not felt the pull of strong emotions?"

—**Michael A. Tompkins,**
San Francisco Bay Area
assistant clinical professor
Berkeley; and coauthor of

"As a certified school psychologist working in high schools for many years, I genuinely wish I had *Parenting a Troubled Teen* to give to the parents and guardians of the students I was helping. Zurita Ona outlines very practical steps for adults who would like to help their teenager thrive during the chaotic times in their lives. Because the book is filled with real-world vignettes and useful exercises, parents and guardians will find *Parenting a Troubled Teen* to be a valuable resource for fostering stronger and more mature relationships."

—**D. J. Moran, PhD, BCBA-D,** founder of Pickslyde Consulting and the MidAmerican Psychological Institute

"As every parent knows, having children brings both joy and pain. But nothing prepares parents for the unique trials and tribulations of a troubled teen. Fortunately, help is at hand. This book is an incredibly practical guide to helping your child reduce suffering, build richer relationships, and become more successful in the face of life's many challenges. No matter how bad things may have gotten, it's never too late to turn the tide; and step-by-step, in a compassionate and respectful way, this book will show you just how to do it."

—**Russ Harris,** author of *The Happiness Trap* and *ACT Made Simple*

"Profound and compassionate, *Parenting a Troubled Teen* affirms real-world tools for caregivers. This book includes important information that offers new possibilities in parenting—challenging assumptions about adolescents while illuminating a fresh perspective on how to forge a meaningful connection that goes beyond 'fixing.'"

> —**Timothy Gordon, MSW, RSW**, social worker, peer-reviewed acceptance and commitment therapy (ACT) trainer, and coauthor of *The ACT Approach*

"Parents of teens who struggle with emotion regulation often describe feeling confused and overwhelmed by their teens' behavior. Zurita Ona has come to the rescue with her beautifully crafted guide on how to apply acceptance and commitment therapy (ACT) to the challenges experienced while parenting highly sensitive teens. This book will help parents manage their own intense emotions, and interact more empathically and effectively with their children. I look forward to recommending this book to the parents of my clients!"

> —**Jamie A. Micco, PhD, ABPP**, clinical psychologist in private practice in Concord, MA, and lecturer in psychology at Harvard Medical School

"If you're parenting a troubled teen, you almost certainly feel like a troubled parent who has a troubled parent-child relationship. If this sounds familiar, read this book! Zurita Ona comes to the rescue with this revolutionary guide for breaking unhelpful patterns of interacting with your teen, becoming the parent you truly aspire to be, and having a rich and meaningful relationship despite the emotional challenges."

> —**Jill A. Stoddard, PhD**, coauthor of *The Big Book of ACT Metaphors*, and director of The Center for Stress and Anxiety Management in San Diego, CA

Parenting a
Troubled Teen

Manage Conflict & Deal with
Intense Emotions Using Acceptance
& Commitment Therapy

PATRICIA E. ZURITA ONA, PSYD

New Harbinger Publications, Inc.

Distributed in Canada by Raincoast Books

Copyright © 2017 by Patricia E. Zurita Ona
      New Harbinger Publications, Inc.
      5674 Shattuck Avenue
      Oakland, CA 94609
      www.newharbinger.com

The exercise "Pure Moments of Purpose" is adapted with permission from MINDFULNESS FOR TWO by Kelly Wilson and Troy DuFrene, copyright © 2008 by Kelly Wilson and Troy DuFrene. Used by permission of New Harbinger Publications, Inc.

Cover design by Amy Shoup

Acquired by Ryan Buresh

Edited by Brady Kahn

All Rights Reserved

Library of Congress Cataloging-in-Publication Data on file

19   18   17

10   9   8   7   6   5   4   3   2   1   First Printing

To my uncles Juan and Franklin, my aunt Sofia,
and my mom, Patricia: you taught me that
life is what we make of it.

To all the parents I worked with:
you have been my greatest teachers.

Contents

PART 4: When Things Get Rocky

Foreword

Relationships are living entities that evolve, morph, and transform, and to be successful, they require attention. No relationship will survive without adjustments, changes, and caring behaviors from the people involved in it. This simple, powerful statement by Patricia Zurita-Ona can dignify even your darkest moments as a parent. This book is written to help you walk that walk and discover the best of yourself, even in the worst moments you will face as a parent. It is a book especially designed for parents of teens with emotion dysregulation problems, those highly sensitive teens who require specialized skills and specialized responses from their parents. Sadly, many parents fail to appreciate this core principle of parenting. Parenting is a process, not an outcome, and success is not determined by heroic, single acts of acceptance or forgiveness, nor by "winning" a heated argument with a teenager. Parenting is a process that is best thought of as a long journey that, unbelievably enough, will bring you to your knees at one juncture and into contact with the best of who you are at another. And this process will go on and on as you and your child travel the path of life together. The journey requires that you persist in being guided by your values as a parent, even as the emotions of the moment tempt you to stop.

Here is another truth from this wonderfully written book: *You cannot choose what shows up under your skin; you cannot choose how your teen feels, thinks, or behaves. But you can choose how to respond in that moment.* In this book, Zurita-Ona is really laying out a serenity prayer for parents. *Know what you can change* (i.e., your behavior in this moment); *know what you must accept* (i.e., your own emotional reactions to your child, memories of your upbringing, self-doubts about your adequacy as a parent, and what your teen says and does to stimulate these things inside of you). And, finally, she offers you a way to self-knowledge: *You possess the wisdom to know the difference.*

Part of this self-knowledge is learning the different types of thoughts that create roadblocks to being true to your values as a parent. The book is written with a format that helps parents to look at their own behaviors that might be driven by either being fused with their internal mind noise or avoiding those uncomfortable emotions themselves. The second part of the book, "Being Real," taps into how the mind comes up with rules, future and past thoughts, stories, and evaluations that only derail parents from having a real relationship with their teen; it teaches parents multiple defusion skills for dealing with each one of those thoughts, images, and memories that show up in their mind.

Here is the central question that life poses in your quest to be the best parent you can be: *When dealing with your teen and feeling triggered by what she's saying or doing, are you willing to have those thoughts, memories, sensations, feelings, and urges, and still do what matters to you as a parent in that particular moment?* This is the essence of the Acceptance and Commitment Therapy approach to parenting: what really matters *to us*. Acceptance is the alternative to the useless struggle to control things in our inner world that can't be controlled. It offers an alternative to using ill-advised strategies that give you momentary relief but backfire in the long run. Emotional pain is not bad for you; instead, it shines a light on what matters to you. Being in the present moment is the alternative to shutting down your emotions and trying to parent your teen at arms-length so you won't get hurt; it presents an alternative to the inward feeling of being rejected or the worry that you are a failure. Zurita-Ona's book is full of easy, practical strategies you can use to help you accept what is going on inside, get present, and be the parent you want to be.

As any parent knows, having the wisdom to respond in a way that will bring you closer to your teen is much easier said than done; standing in the way is your own reluctance to feel what you feel, think what you think, remember what you remember, and sense what you sense inside. There is a chapter specifically written for fathers or male caregivers because societal rules about how to be a man do not necessarily drive effective parenting behaviors. Remember that the journey of parenting is really an inward-looking process catalyzed by this annoying life force you brought into the world. There is an old saying that makes another important point about parenting: *It takes two to tango.* You and your teen's behaviors are inextricably linked and are keyed in with each other. As Zurita-Ona points out, as human beings, you are both actually seeking the same thing: *At the root of your emotional needs, your teen's emotional needs, and every human being's emotional needs, there is the same need for affection, caring, acceptance, forgiveness, and love.* Wouldn't it be awesome if you could bring that thought along with you when you are tempted to kill your teen! *Hey! You are both seeking the same thing; it is not about winning this battle of wills. It is about figuring out a way to have us both get to that place of mutual affection, acceptance, and love.* This book will give you a tool chest of practical strategies for getting you and your teen to that place. It is not about validating your teen's behaviors; it is about finding ways to appreciate and empathize with your teen's struggle. It is also about helping you find forgiveness and compassion for yourself as the parent of a teen who struggles with emotional dyregulation. There is often a need for parents to let go of the guilt they carry inside.

There is a long-standing theory about parenting that I would recommend you strongly adhere to, and it oozes out of the pores of this book. *It is not about being a perfect parent; there aren't any of those on this planet. It is about being a good enough parent.* Being a *good enought parent* is about remembering that even though you made mistakes along the way, your intentions were honorable and you did enough good things to give your teen a chance to succeed in the world. You don't have to do everything right to be the parent you want to be. In some senses, parenting is a form of judo; you take the negative energy of the moment and transform it into an opportunity for compassion toward yourself and your teen. This way, you can lean in to your pain and your teen's pain, rather than resist it. And, by the way, even if your teen never says a word about this move of acceptance and self-love, he or she is watching your every move and will emulate you in the future!

—Kirk D. Strosahl, PhD
coauthor of *Brief Interventions for Radical Change* and
the *Mindfulness and Acceptance Workbook for Depression*

Introduction

This is not a theoretical book, and it's not written from the office of a researcher. This book is the direct result of my clinical experience, first as an educational psychologist and later on as a clinical psychologist, working with teens, parents, and families affected by mild to severe emotion dysregulation problems in one form or another.

My work with those parents has been one of the most rewarding experiences I have ever had. Supporting them to navigate from really challenging places, when they were afraid for the lives of their teens, to sweet moments of connection and laughter with their teens has been a true gift. I'm eternally grateful for the families who walked into my therapy office and worked so hard moment by moment in their lives. I wouldn't have been able to write this book without the experiences they shared, their trust in me, and the challenges we navigated together.

I respect what parents do and appreciate what they go through on a daily basis when raising a highly sensitive teen. One moment you are looking at your baby in your arms, and the next one he's a teen screaming at you. I know the gap between the dream you may have had for your teen, all the work you put into materializing that dream, and the reality of discovering that your teen struggles with emotion dysregulation.

Life brings all types of challenges to us, and we don't see them coming at times. It's life, and the business of being alive is not easy, but what's the alternative when all types of struggles unexpectedly hit us? What's the alternative when you don't understand what's going on with your teen despite all the love you have for him? Do you give up? Do you stoically tell yourself that you should embrace your pain? Do you tell yourself you should learn about it? Our minds naturally come up with many problem-solving strategies, but our pain is our pain, and our reality gap is our reality gap.

Here is what I have learned: we continue to search for what matters to us, our life treasure, and we make the best of every moment we have. In the end, life brings to us not only pain but also beautiful, sweet moments of connection and an invitation to choose how to live our life given where things are and how they are.

This book is an invitation for you to choose the parent you want to be when raising your teen with emotion dysregulation struggles. You require a specialized set of skills, and acceptance and commitment therapy (ACT) can make a difference for you. ACT (pronounced as a single word) is an empirically supported treatment approach based on a psychological theory of language known as relational frame theory (RFT) and has been researched in 136 randomized clinical trials, the most rigorous type of scientific research (Hayes 2016).

I did my best when writing this book, and now I want to invite you to continue giving your best for your teen while you learn new skills that will help. My best wishes to you in this journey of ACTifying your parenting skills!

PART 1

Getting Started

CHAPTER 1

"Why Is It so Hard?": How ACT Can Help

Have you ever had your teen go from being calm one minute to screaming the next because you asked him to come back home by 10:00 p.m.? What about waiting for your teen to come down to breakfast and then finding cuts on her wrists? Did you find your teen crying in her bedroom, refusing to talk to anyone for hours or even days because no one replied to her post in Facebook? Has your teen ever been talking about how school was going, until you offered some advice about a project, and then he suddenly began yelling at you? All those behaviors in your teen are indications of emotion dysregulation problems. This chapter will help you get a firmer grip on what is going on for your teen and for you.

Emotion dysregulation is a chain of intense emotional reactions to a situation that is too much, too quick, and too soon for that particular situation; it is as if your teen has an emotional switch that quickly turns on and off at any time. Teens struggling with emotion dysregulation experience their emotions at a very intense level because of their sensitivity, and when they are hurt or upset, it feels like an open wound. In those moments of high emotionality, they engage in all type of behaviors, problematic ones for the most part, to respond, suppress, or diminish their difficult feelings as quickly as possible. Common problematic responses include lashing out, disconnecting, blaming, name-calling, or threatening; these behavioral responses are challenging for both the teens experiencing them and the people around them. A parent on the receiving end, like yourself, only sees a teen switching quickly from being okay to being extremely upset, and it's hard to make sense of what happened in between the upsetting situation and your teen's response.

When a Teen Feels Too Much, Too Quick, Too Soon

A fifteen-year-old teen described emotion dysregulation problems as "feeling like a house on fire. Everything feels intense, as if you're burning inside and you don't know how to calm the fire. Nothing makes sense. You can't think clearly. You only feel the fire burning you."

Adolescence is already a complex and vulnerable developmental stage, but having emotion dysregulation problems makes things even more difficult. To start, it's as if your teen were a prisoner of his reactions, not only to one emotion but to almost all emotions: when he is anxious, he's extremely anxious; when feeling sad, he's overwhelmed with sadness; when he's frustrated, he's very frustrated; when he's happy, he's very happy. When these emotions are activated, you will hear a lot of black-and-white thinking, where it's all one way or the other in the mind of the teen and there's no room for compromise. For instance, if you were to ask your son to go to a family gathering, he might say, "If I go to spend time with your family, I don't want you to tell me what's appropriate or not for me to say to them." Conversations escalate really quickly without you being able to detect what's happening.

When high emotionality is on a roll, there is a gap between how a problem became a problem and the intensity of your teen's reaction. From one day to the next, your teen may become best friends with someone she met only once or twice, or she may quickly stop being friends with a classmate who didn't respond to her texts the same day. While situations like these may seem typical for teenagers, if you look closely, you'll find it's part of a larger pattern in which your teen's responses tend to go from one extreme to another, not just with you or at home but also with friends and at school. Being prone to emotional sensitivity and reactivity makes teens victims of emotional hijacking; their lives quickly unfold into multiple angry episodes, self-harm behaviors, and even attempts at suicide. It's not easy for them, and it's not easy for you.

Most emotionally dysregulated teens notice that situations can set them off really quickly, but they don't fully understand what's happening to them; it may be only years later that they realize their responses are not within the range of what most people experience.

How Parents Get Triggered Too

For you, the parent or caregiver, witnessing your teen's emotion dys-regulation problems is not easy. As one parent told me, "I don't have a clue as to what happened. I simply asked my daughter to pick up her clothes from the floor, and the next thing I knew, she was screaming at me about how I don't understand her." You experience high levels of stress, and without realizing it, you may also be hijacked by your emotions, including having troublesome thoughts about parenting and intense physical reactions, when you're dealing with your teenager. Because of the intensity of these experiences, you may engage in certain strategies to manage your own internal experience and start parenting based on those strategies. Sometimes those parenting strategies work, and sometimes they don't. The biggest challenge comes when you get triggered as much as your teen does, basically responding to reactivity with reactivity, which simply makes the situation worse for both of you.

This book offers a different approach to take when dealing with those moments in which the emotional switch is on for both of you.

Change is possible. Being the parent you want to be is possible, and helping your teen without damaging your relationship is possible. Acceptance and commitment therapy (ACT) can help you facilitate this process of change.

How ACT Can Make a Difference

Acceptance and commitment therapy was developed by Hayes, Strosahl, and Wilson (1999), and it's based on relational frame theory of language (Hayes, Barnes-Holmes, and Roche 2001). A form of cognitive behavioral therapy, ACT currently has 136 randomized clinical trials demonstrating its applicability and efficacy in the treatment of multiple psychological struggles (Hayes 2016).

ACT invites you to do three things: accept, choose, and take action in your parenting life. When applying ACT into your parenting life, you're invited to first *accept* your internal experiences—thoughts, memories, emotions, sensations, and urges you have when dealing with your teen—in particular when they are uncomfortable, by learning to let them be, without trying to change, alter, or deny them; second, *choose* what truly matters to you as a parent by identifying and recognizing your individual parenting values; and finally, *take* specific behavioral actions toward those parenting values in your daily life.

By practicing acceptance, choosing intentionally your values, and taking action toward becoming the parent you want to be, you will discover a new experience: a parenting life that is full of meaning and growth. ACT doesn't offer you a perfect parenting life that is free of conflict, but it certainly invites you to stop going in circles and get unstuck with your teen.

Why ACT?

In traditional parenting classes, training, coaching sessions, or even self-help books, you are often asked to identify your goals. While establishing your goals may look initially useful, it falls short in helping you deal with the unique struggles of your teen's emotion dysregulation problems and the larger picture of your parenting role: who do you want to be as parent?

ACT invites you to choose your parenting values and, in taking actions that are based on those values, find a sense of purpose and direction in your parenting life that is beyond traditional parenting goals. Learning and applying ACT skills to handle your teen is likely to be more powerful for you as a parent and for your relationship with your teen than using other approaches.

How to Read This Book

This book is structured into four parts. The first part, "Getting Started" (which you are reading now), provides you with an introduction to ACT. It invites you to look at all the parenting strategies you have been relying on to manage your teen's behavior.

The second part, "Being Real," is all about learning to pay attention to the nitty-gritty moments of your internal experience when parenting your teen. You will identify the different types of thoughts, memories, emotions, impulses, and sensations that show up for you and learn how to handle them in a way that makes room for you to choose your parenting response; at the end of each chapter, a section called "weekly practice" will give you exercises to reinforce your skills and your commitment to being the parent you want to be.

The third part, "Making a Shift," teaches you some ACT parenting skills that will help you move forward. These include mindfulness, appreciation, empathy, assertiveness, behavioral management, conflict resolution, how to deal with anger, forgiveness, and compassion skills.

The last part, "When Things Get Rocky," addresses what to do in those challenging moments when things go wrong even when you've done your best. Chapter 18 is especially written for fathers or male caregivers who are dealing with a teen's emotional-sensitivity problems. Finally, the appendix addresses suicidal or parasuicidal behaviors, problematic eating behaviors, and substance abuse issues.

Some chapter topics may speak to you more than others, and you may be inclined to skip around, but you will benefit more from reading the chapters in order since each chapter builds on what comes before it. Also, as you work your way through this book, it will be helpful to keep a parenting journal, since many of the exercises involve writing.

Are you ready to ACTify your parenting skills? Let's start by looking at what you're already doing to try to help your emotionally dysregulated teen. That's the topic of the next chapter.

CHAPTER 2

"My House Is a Stress Machine": Your Struggle as a Parent

It's Monday night, and Kathleen returns home after a long day at work. She opens the door, and as soon as she enters, her fifteen-year-old daughter, Natalie, calls out, "Can I spend the night at Chad's house?"

Caught by surprise, Kathleen pauses, and says, "You were there all weekend. It's Monday, and it's a school week—"

Kathleen is unable to finish the sentence before Natalie yells back at her, "If you don't let me go to Chad's, I'm gonna be depressed, and then I'm gonna cut!"

Kathleen raises her voice too. "You know you can't go to Chad's tonight. Why do you do this to me?"

Natalie starts screaming and runs upstairs to her bedroom. Next, Kathleen begins to cry; she doesn't know whether she should go upstairs or not. She starts yelling while running up the stairs; she pounds on Natalie's door, asking Natalie to open it, but there is no response.

When Kathleen came back home and encountered the situation described above with her fifteen-year-old daughter, she did the best she could to handle the situation in that particular moment. She said no and tried to explain why; she tried to be firm and quickly found herself screaming. Arguments like this happen more often than not in Kathleen's household. Any denial of a request from Natalie can easily escalate into a battle of wills, with threats, tears, and doors slamming. While Kathleen is doing her best, her relationship with Natalie seems to be getting only worse. Kathleen feels hopeless about the situation, and Natalie continues to become an island.

Does this scenario sound familiar to you? If you have a teen at home who struggles with emotional sensitivity, you know it's as if he has an emotional switch that suddenly turns on—his reactions are too strong, too quick, too often. Sometimes you can anticipate when the emotional switch will turn on; other times it happens so suddenly, like a fire alarm going off, that you are caught off guard and end up thoroughly confused about what just happened. Naturally, you try to calm these emotional flare-ups using every strategy that you believe will help your teen calm down, and of course, that's totally understandable. After all, what are you supposed to do when your teen is totally out of control?

In the next few pages, I'm going to invite you to take a close look at those difficult situations with your teen and begin to discover better ways to support him when his emotional switch is on. You cannot make the situation better unless you look at it more closely.

Let's Play Detective: Your Responses

A detective usually carries a first-rate magnifying glass to see things in fine detail. Like a detective, you will pay close attention to the types of memories, thoughts, sensations, emotions, and urges that you have experienced in the midst of these challenging situations with your teen. And just to make sure we're on the same page, keep in mind that when looking at thoughts, we will be looking at the words, images, and memories that show up in your mind; also, the terms *feelings* and *emotions* will be used interchangeably throughout the book; and finally, an *urge* or *impulse* is what you feel like doing based on the thought, emotion, or sensation you're having.

EXERCISE: Recall a Difficult Situation You Had with Your Teen

Let's figure out what's going on when dealing with your teen during times in which his emotional switch has been turned on. Recall a difficult situation that you had with your teen in the past week or so. Do your best to imagine this moment vividly, zooming in on the details.

With this specific situation in mind, pull out your parenting journal, and write down your answers to these questions.

1. What was the triggering event (what caused the situation)?

2. What did you go through internally? Write about the thoughts, images, feelings, and physical sensations you had at the time.

3. How did you respond to the situation?

When Kathleen completed this exercise, her responses looked like this:

1. Triggering event: *Natalie asking to spend the night with her boyfriend*

2. Internal thoughts, feelings, sensations: *Why does she need to ask me this today? Doesn't she know it's not okay? I have told her many times she cannot sleep at Chad's home on the weekdays. What's wrong with her? Why does she try to control the situation? Feeling very frustrated.*

3. Response to the situation: *Explain why she cannot go. Then scream at her.*

After you have zoomed in on the specifics of a problematic situation, you can take an even closer look at it. Answer two more questions:

1. What happens to your teen's behavior in the moment (what does your teen do)?

2. What happens to you in that moment?

If Kathleen were answering these new questions, her answers would look like this:

Natalie runs to her bedroom; she screams back at me and threatens to cut her wrist. I feel exhausted. Am crying, feeling helpless, not knowing what to do next.

After looking at this difficult situation, did you notice that in that moment, you and your teen are each managing your own emotions, sensations, images, memories, and thoughts? You have to deal with your internal private noise when your teen does or says something that is upsetting to you, and simultaneously, your teen has to deal with his own private noise when you respond the way you respond.

If you step back from the conflict to examine it, you may see that your teen's behavior is a trigger for you, and your response becomes a trigger for your teen. In that particular moment of struggle, it is really as though you and your teen were dancing together, but instead of dancing together in a synchronized manner, you are stepping on each other's feet.

Sometimes parents tell me, "But Patricia, it works! When I scream back to my teen, he stops." Giving it back to your teen in equal measure may seem to work in the moment. However, it does nothing to stop the problematic behavior in the long run. You are both responding to each other with what you have learned about handling conflict, but that doesn't mean that what you are doing is helpful to your relationship. If these interactions reoccur a number of times, ask yourself whether this type of response is really helping the two of you to get closer or is actually making things worse in the long term.

You're Trying Too Hard

By now you may have tried a variety of strategies in an effort to manage your teen's problematic behavior. You may have already read many parenting books, taken your teen to therapists, offered him money, removed his cell phone, forbidden him to see his friends, taken away his ability to buy music from iTunes, and so on.

EXERCISE: What Have You Tried?

Take out your parenting journal and create a list of everything you have done to manage your teen's behavior; label this list "strategies." Then looking at each strategy, ask yourself if that strategy has brought you closer to the parent you want to be. Write down your response next to that strategy. Then write down what happens to your relationship with your teen when you've used that strategy in the past.

Here are some examples:

Strategy: *Offer money if he behaves*

Does doing this bring you closer to the parent you want to be? *No.*

What happens to your relationship with your teen? *Gets worse.*

Strategy: *Giving up on asking for compliance*

Does doing this bring you closer to the parent you want to be? *No.*

What happens to your relationship with your teen? *He still gets angry at me.*

Strategy: *Yelling at him*

Does doing this bring you closer to the parent you want to be? *No.*

What happens to your relationship with your teen? *He screams back. Complains to his grandmother about me.*

Strategy: *Saying firmly, "Stop and listen."*

Does doing this bring you closer to the parent you want to be? *No.*

What happens to your relationship with your teen? *He criticizes everything I do, even if it's unrelated to him.*

Be as specific as possible with your list, especially when you write about what happens to your relationship with your teen when you use each strategy. Afterward, write down anything you noticed as you were taking this inventory. Looking back at the inventory, are any of your parenting strategies working?

If you completed this inventory, kudos to you. You have successfully accomplished what many parents cannot do, which is to look at your parenting strategies. What did you notice when completing this inventory? Did you make any discoveries? At this point, you may have realized that when you are triggered by your teen's problematic behaviors and respond to them in the best way you can while managing your own internal private noise; some of the parenting strategies you have used certainly work in the moment but they are often not sustainable in the long run.

Allow me to clarify that I am not suggesting that you are a bad parent or that you should let your teen get away with whatever he wants to do because he threatens you. What I am suggesting is that the difficult moments you and your teen go through cannot be understood in isolation but need to be understood within the context of how the two of you interact when you are both feeling triggered. You are both hurting in those moments: not just you, not just him.

Sometimes when I have this conversation with parents, they ask, "Why do I have to do all the heavy lifting? Why do I have to work so hard with my teen? He should just be doing what teens are supposed to do. He should be going along with what his parents say." I never have a perfect response for these questions. I would like to have an answer for why a teen behaves in a certain way or another, but I don't. I wish your teen would simply go along with anything you request from him, but that's not the case, and you can't control his behavior.

I can tell you that while understandably and naturally you may feel that you should not have to work so hard to have a healthy relationship with your teen and that your teen should go along with whatever you say, these wishful thoughts are just another attempt to manage his behavior. Sorry, but there is no way to guarantee that your teen will respond positively to every instruction you give him, and there is no therapy, medication, or self-help book that will make it happen. All relationships require a certain amount of work, including this one with your teen.

If you continue to read this book, you will find tools to help you stop parenting behaviors that hurt the relationship with your teen and tools to help you effectively handle stressful situations that will inevitably occur. As you change your behavior, your teen's behavior will change too. At times it may feel like a long road, yet change is possible. There is no guarantee, of course, but it does happen.

If things get very rocky at some point, such as if you fear for your own safety or your teen's safety, then, without a doubt, it will be time to switch strategies (as suggested in the appendix). If you choose to switch strategies, then at least you will know that you gave it your best shot.

On the other hand, if you're unwilling to try anything different from what you've been doing fruitlessly up until now, then it's quite likely that the relationship with your teen could simply go from bad to worse.

Making the Shift

If you are open to continuing to look at what you go through internally when dealing with a problematic situation with your teen, and you are willing to acknowledge that you both engage in a chain of behaviors that trigger each other—even though you are not the one who started the chain—then there is room for this book to be helpful to you.

You've already made great progress. You've looked closely at how you respond to conflicts with your teen. You've also identified and examined the effectiveness of all the strategies you've used in an attempt to manage his behavior. As a last exercise in this chapter, it will be helpful to look at your perceptions of your teen when the two of you are in conflict and to consider the impact of those perceptions on your relationship.

Exercise: What You Think When You're in Conflict

Think of a recent conflict or series of conflicts that you've had with your teen. Grab your parenting journal so you can examine what you think about your teen when you are in conflict. Keep in mind that this exercise is a private one, only for you, and there is no need to edit your thoughts. Take the following steps.

1. Write down all the thoughts (criticisms, judgments, complaints) you have about your teen when you're in a conflict with him.

2. Now imagine you are in your teen's shoes, and start reading those thoughts slowly, one by one.

3. Imagine what it must be like for your teen to be on the receiving end of all those thoughts you have about him.

4. Slowly notice any reaction you may be having right now. Are any memories or thoughts showing up? Any emotions? Any impulses? Any physical sensations? Write down your reactions.

Did you notice how your thoughts about your teen have an impact on your ability to handle conflict with your teen?

Those criticisms, negative judgments, and complaints you have about your teen are very real, and I'm sure there are many experiences that have led you to have them. At the same time, looking at a conflict with your teen through the lens of those criticisms, judgments, and complaints doesn't allow you to see that he's hurting in that moment, just as you are, and see that the way that you both handle conflict has been ineffective for the relationship.

What's Getting in the Way of Making a Shift?

If when completing the previous exercise, your mind was coming up with thoughts such as *He doesn't care. He's responsible for everything. I gave him everything I could*, then you have two options. One option is to continue dwelling on how bad your teen is; if you choose to do this, the result will be only more conflict and increasing distance between the two of you.

The other option is to let your mind simply acknowledge these thoughts for the time being and then ask yourself if those particular thoughts help you or not in handling conflict with your teen. Choosing this option doesn't mean that all of those critical thoughts about your teen will suddenly go away. In fact, thoughts along the lines of *My teen is a bad kid* will fight for survival, emerge over and over again, and you may have to ask yourself again and again whether that narrative gets you closer to your teen or not. Choosing this second option comes with a big bonus for you: over time you will learn how to respond to your teen in ways that will improve the relationship.

Your teen may have never spoken to you about what is going on, or when he did start to talk about it, the conversation may have gotten heated and you both started arguing. We know that many teens are not skillful at telling parents, adults, or even other teens about their struggles. In fact, the most common response for teens is to hide their pain the best they can. They hide their troubles, not because they don't want to get help or because they want to keep things from you but because talking about their difficulties makes them feel very vulnerable. I still recall a teen with whom I worked years ago who was referred to my practice because of cutting behaviors. After weeks of working together, she confided that she was having flashbacks from being bullied at school and that she had learned to cope with those intense memories and feelings by cutting her wrists. No one knew about her struggles at school. Her parents discovered she was cutting only after finding tissue paper with blood in the trash can.

When you make a positive shift in your parenting behavior, you may begin to notice a positive shift in your teen's behavior as well. The more you read this book, the more equipped you will be with different ACT skills to handle rocky moments with your teen. Ultimately, this book is about helping you be the best parent you can possibly be. Are you ready to start this new journey?

PART 2

Being Real

CHAPTER 3

"She's so Manipulative": Judgment Thoughts

Peter is getting ready to leave for work and is waiting for his teenage daughter Stella to come downstairs, so he can drive her to school. He's been waiting ten minutes already, and despite his calling up to her several times, she has not come down to have breakfast with the rest of the family. Peter feels frustrated and doesn't understand why it always takes her so long to do something as simple as getting ready to go to school. Then he hears footsteps, and turning to look at her, he sees that Stella is still in her pajamas. Taken aback, he asks, "Why aren't you ready? We are leaving in ten minutes."

She looks at him and says, "Dad, I don't feel well. I need to stay home."

Peter's immediate reaction is one of concern that she is getting sick. But then he notices her pupils are bloodshot like she's high on marijuana. He raises his voice, "Have you been smoking?"

She replies, "No dad. I'm just sick and need to stay home. Come on, haven't you ever been sick?"

Now Peter can smell the marijuana, so he asks again, "Have you been smoking? Tell me the truth."

Stella starts to scream, "You don't love me! You've never loved me!" and she runs back upstairs. Peters runs after her and finds the end of a joint in her trash can.

Peter was frustrated, upset, and disappointed when he caught his teen in such a bold-faced lie. When he went to work

*that day, he couldn't stop thinking about what just happened. He
asked himself, Why did she lie to me? What happened to my
kid? She's so manipulative. She's always trying to get away with
whatever she can. She has become so selfish. It's all about her.*

You may sympathize with Peter's feelings. Chances are you've
had similar thoughts about your teen. It's normal. It's natural. You're
not a bad parent for having those thoughts. Like Peter, you probably
think you didn't raise your teen to behave the way she does.

It's completely understandable to go into a moment of mental
shock when you are confronted with the fact that your teen is not
that same little child whom you held in your arms because she was
afraid of the dark and who asked you to stay with her until she fell
asleep. Your child has grown into a teen and is still growing, and in
this process, there are moments that are extremely hard for you,
similar to what Peter went through when he caught his daughter
lying to him, straight faced. Parenting a teen with emotion dysregulation problems is tough work.

Noticing Judgment Thoughts

All the thoughts that Peter had about Stella, that she's a liar, manipulative, and selfish, are evaluations of Stella; those evaluations are
called *judgment thoughts* and can be positive or negative, good or
bad; our mind naturally comes up with them all the time about
objects, situations, experiences, or people. The ability to evaluate,
classify, criticize, and judge is unique to human beings, and we're
evolutionarily wired to do it; our early ancestors learned to differen-
tiate what's good from what's bad so they could put their efforts
toward preventing anything bad from happening. No human being
is exempt from our evaluative minds.

To see how the mind naturally judges, try this exercise right
now. Simply walk into your teen's room and slowly notice every
thought that crosses your mind, then write them down in your
parenting journal. If you cannot walk into your teen's room, then
simply imagine her room, notice what thoughts quickly come to
mind, and write them down. Chances are your mind may have come

up with all types of judgments, both positive and negative, about your teen's room and even about her. As you will learn in this chapter and throughout this book, judgment thoughts, like any other thoughts, constantly show up like windows popping up on your computer screen.

The problem is not the fact that we have these evaluative thoughts but the way that we handle them in our daily lives. We have been taught to believe in every single thought that comes up and behave as if those thoughts were the absolute truth. The challenge is that most of these thoughts are far from being real, because our minds are constantly active as if they had lives of their own. Certainly some of those thoughts are true, and we call these true thoughts facts, but most of them are just mind-talk in the form of wishes, assumptions, expectations, dreams, ideas, and so on.

Our mind is constantly doing its job, coming up with all types of mental noise as if it had a life of its own. However, from just having those thoughts in your mind to actually believing every one of them and acting on each one of them, there is a stretch. Within ACT, holding all thoughts as absolute truth and confusing them with reality is called *cognitive fusion*. Cognitive fusion, or getting "fused, hooked, or caught up" on your thoughts, is believing that every thought, memory, or image that shows up in your mind is real and quickly giving these thoughts all your attention, latching on to them, dwelling, and stewing on them. Getting fused so quickly in those criticisms, evaluations, and judgment thoughts makes it harder for any parent to step back and choose how to respond to a given situation in a helpful manner or based on what's really important to you. For instance, following Peter's example, after continually buying into judgment thoughts about Stella being a liar, manipulative, and selfish, he decided to not talk to her for a week. At dinnertime, Stella, still in pajamas, tried to talk to him, but he acted as if she didn't exist. The same pattern repeated itself for the next six days. Peter acted as if his judgment thoughts were absolute truths; he was fused with and trapped by these thoughts.

While it's understandable that Peter behaved as he did and that his mind would come up with those judgment thoughts, not talking to Stella for a week was an ineffective response to the situation, didn't improved his relationship with her, and was a departure from what's really important to him as parent.

Wait...Wait...It's True

Sometimes when discussing the idea that it's natural to have judgment thoughts and that they are simply thoughts—not necessarily absolute truths—parents say things like "But my teen really is a slob. You haven't seen her bedroom. It's ridiculous. There is food all over the night table, clothes all over the floor." And they're right. I haven't seen the teen's bedroom. However, I would add that when your mind comes with a criticism about your teen, and you have the urge to do X, the question to ask is, "Would this action you want to take serve to escalate or de-escalate the conflict?" Notice that I'm not asking whether the judgment thought is true or not but asking whether if behaving based on that particular judgment thought is helpful or not in that given moment. Parents usually recognize that when having those criticisms about their teens, they feel like screaming at them, removing all privileges immediately for the rest of the year, and so on, but later acknowledge that behaving that way simply escalates the conflict.

I personally know how difficult it is to step back and answer the question of whether the actions I take, based on judgment thoughts, are helpful or not in a particular situation. I also know that, although difficult, it's possible. We all struggle with making a choice when triggered; however, we can also learn to step back and check in with ourselves whether our behavior will make things better or worse for us in a given moment.

EXERCISE: Taking a Judgment Inventory

Let's take a look at one of those moments in which you felt like killing your teen—yes, you read that right, and as bad as it might sound, most parents experience those moments. It's natural. Be as honest as possible with yourself. Please think about the terrible times you've had with your teen and jot down in your journal all the judgment thoughts, evaluations, and criticisms that may have shown up in your mind about her.

Then, complete the sentence *My mind says my teen is...*with each of the judgment thoughts, evaluations, and criticisms on your list. When Peter did this exercise, his list looked like this:

My mind says that my teen is...a liar; irrational, manipulative, very selfish; she only thinks about herself.

My mind says that my teen is...a drama queen, an angry teen, unmotivated.

My mind says that my teen is...out of control.

Notice any reaction you had during or after completing this sentence. Any apprehension about writing down those judgment thoughts? If so, you are not alone. Your parenting mind is doing its job; it naturally evaluates, judges, criticizes, and classifies.

Acknowledging and accepting that at times your mind comes up with these evaluative thoughts about your teen is a beginning. Recognizing that your mind, like my mind and anyone's mind, quickly could become a judgment machine is simply being honest.

Old psychology books, including academic and self-help books, often present the idea that having negative judgments, criticisms, or evaluations is bad and that we must hide, deny, or challenge them, as if your mind could have only positive judgments. As an experiment to evaluate whether we can suppress or eliminate our negative judgments, I invite you right now to not think about a dark piece of chocolate.

Now, what just happened? If your mind is like mine, as soon as I asked you to not think about a dark piece of chocolate, you had the image of it. Telling yourself to avoid judgment thoughts won't work; in fact, research has suggested that ongoing efforts to suppress, deny, eliminate, or push them away will simply increase their frequency.

As long as we're alive, our minds will spontaneously come up with hundreds of judgments, criticisms, and evaluations throughout the day, as if our mind carried what I call a *judgment machine*. Here's a quick exercise inspired by an exercise in Harris (2009) that illustrates how the judgment machine works.

EXERCISE: The Judgment Machine

Simply practice right where you are by taking the following steps:

1. Bring to your mind all those judgment thoughts about your teen.

2. Place your hands together in front of you, palms upward, like an open book.

3. Then imagine placing each judgment thought onto a finger. Say the thoughts out loud as you place them on each finger. For instance, your thumb could be "She is a liar," your index finger "She is manipulative," and so on, until you have labeled each finger with a judgment about your teen.

4. Slowly raise your hands up toward your face until they are covering your eyes.

5. Notice whether you can see the room or not.

6. Bring your hands back down into your lap.

What did you notice? Were you able to see the room or only parts of it? Now imagine if your teen were standing in front of you. Would you be able to see your teen for who she is, or would you be looking at your teen through this judgment machine?

If you continue to get caught up in your judgment thoughts, you will be unable to see your teen for who she is. Again, getting caught up or fused in those evaluative thoughts, believing and behaving as though they were the absolute truth about your teen, not only affects how you feel in the moment but also impacts how you feel about your teen, how you see your teen, and how you respond to your teen when a conflict arrives.

So if you can't eliminate judgment thoughts, because our minds naturally carry a judgment machine, what can you do to stop being fused to the evaluations and criticisms that your mind produces about your teen?

Describing: An Antidote to Judgments

All of us have our own judgment machine working at maximum capacity most of the time, but when we get fused to the evaluations and criticisms that it produces, we foreclose a simple but important ability: to describe what we see. Describing situations, experiences, objects, and others' behaviors for what they are allows us to get unhooked from our judgment machine long enough to make a big difference in how we respond to those judgments. Describing is simply stating what you see for what it is, as if you were a witness in a courtroom. When you describe what happens, you simply report what you see without adding an interpretation.

Finding an opportunity to switch from judging to describing is as easy as looking around wherever you are and noticing what you see. As an exercise, look at your surroundings in this moment, choose an object, and notice what your mind says about it. If your mind comes up with such terms as *ugly*, *bad*, *pretty*, *cute*, *dirty*, or *pleasant*, then your judgment machine is on. See if instead you can simply describe the attributes of that object. Here is an example: I noticed a chair in my living room, and my mind naturally came up with the judgment *ugly*. When I looked at it again and made a choice to describe the chair's attributes, I came up with this: *The fabric of the chair is blue velvet, soft, lumpy, and the chair has wooden legs.*

From this example, you can see how describing and judging are very different mental tasks. Returning to Peter's example, if he were asked to pause, notice the judgments he had about Stella—that she's selfish—and then simply describe what he had observed without judgment, he might say, "When going into the kitchen and preparing herself a sandwich, she didn't ask her brother whether he wanted a sandwich too."

EXERCISE: Practice Describing

To practice distinguishing descriptions from evaluations, choose a particular negative judgment thought your mind has about your teen and see if you can come up with a description of your teen's behavior that's related to the judgment. When Peter completed this exercise, he came up with these judgment thoughts and descriptions:

Judgment thought: *Stella is lazy.*

Description: *Stella doesn't get up until 9:30 a.m.*

Judgment thought: *Stella is manipulative.*

Description: *Stella does whatever she needs to get what she wants. If I say no to a request, then she asks her mom, or she will text me multiple times asking the same question in different ways.*

What happened when you switched from judging to describing your teen's behavior? Did you have any trouble describing without judging the behavior? If so, you will have plenty of other opportunities to practice this new skill.

Describing is a very important skill, and throughout this book, you will be asked to describe your teen's or your own behavior as a starting point to many of the exercises that are covered. It's quite likely that even when you're intentionally describing a situation, object, or your teen's behavior, your mind will play tricks and quickly turn on the judgment machine, and the judgment machine will, in turn, loudly push you to react and take action. Within ACT you're invited to pause, notice those judgment thoughts, and then choose how to handle them. Learning to step back from our judgment thoughts in a given moment is called *defusion*.

Defusion: A Survival Skill

Defusion is a core ACT skill you can use to handle the many difficult thoughts your parenting mind comes up with. What you choose to do with all of those sticky thoughts is the key, and defusion will allow you to step back, get some distance from your thoughts, accept them for what they are, and give yourself a chance to choose how to respond to them instead of just quickly reacting.

Here is how to practice defusion: first, you notice when the judgment machine gets activated. Next, name all those evaluations, judgments, or criticizing thoughts as a theme; you can name them any name you want, including silly names, or you can simply notice what your mind is doing by saying silently *criticizing, judging, evaluating.* Peter named his judgment thoughts "dangerous thoughts." Another parent I worked with named her thoughts "Ms. Self-righteous." Naming the thought for what it is allows you to step back from it. Again, having a thought, including these very loud judgment thoughts, doesn't mean that you have to act on it. Here's another defusion exercise.

EXERCISE: Clouds in the Sky

Think of different judgment thoughts that your judgment machine has about your teen; then imagine that every time you notice a judgment thought, you place it inside a cloud that is floating on the sky. You can clearly see the font, color, and even size of those judgment thoughts inside the cloud; and now watch the cloud carrying your judgment thought slowly moving through the sky until it fades from your sight.

After completing this defusion exercise, do you see the difference between noticing these judgment thoughts and acting on them? Having a thought, including these very loud judgment thoughts, doesn't mean that you have to act on them.

The more you practice defusion, the more you will learn to have all types of thoughts and then choose your behavioral response; this may seem impossible at the beginning, but as Victor Frankl said, "Between stimulus and response there is a space. In that space is our power to choose our response." Defusion is a key skill in your parenting job, because instead of responding to your teen's reactivity with reactivity, as Peter did, it allows you to respond to your teen's emotional sensitivity based on what's really important to you.

Here is one more defusion exercise to try: after naming your judgment thoughts, you can acknowledge and appreciate that your mind is simply doing its job. For example, you could say, *Thank you, judgment machine* or *Thank you, Ms. Self-righteous.* At the end, your mind is simply doing what it is wired to do, which is coming up with evaluations and criticisms, as all minds do.

Some of the parents I work with try to replace each criticizing thought with a positive one as a way to counter the critical thoughts; the challenge is that this replacement strategy may work but only in the short term, because it's only a matter of time that your mind, like my mind, will come up again with another judgment thought. Pushing against judgment thoughts or any attempts to replace them is still getting fused and hooked on those thoughts, because you're still paying attention to them.

With defusion, you can learn to notice and acknowledge judgment thoughts without doing anything besides choosing your parenting response. Even when things are getting heated with your teen, defusing from your judgment machine and putting it aside will give you a moment of choice to handle those evaluative thoughts instead of automatically behaving in a reactive way.

Summary

The judgment machine is wired within our minds, and it simply does its job throughout our life. This only becomes problematic when we become fused with our criticisms, evaluations, or judgment thoughts and respond to them as if they were absolute truths. Most of us can easily get hooked on our judgment machine in the middle of a difficult situation and subsequently toss out any skill we have learned. However, taking that road will only increase the distance between you and your teen and make things worse for the two of you. Describing your teen's behavior for what it is, noticing whether the judgment machine is on or not, and then defusing from it, will make a difference not only in handling conflict with your teen but also in improving the overall quality of your relationship with her.

Defusion is a crucial skill within ACT and will allow you to notice criticisms and all types of thoughts, create distance from them, and give you a chance to choose your behavioral response to a particular situation with your teen.

Weekly Practice: Defusing from Judgments

This book will present a number of different defusion exercises, and some may naturally resonate with you more than others. My invitation to you is to try them all. Just as you cannot learn to walk by reading about walking—you actually have to walk—you cannot learn ACT skills by reading about them; you have to practice them.

Try out two different defusion exercises this week. First, on a flash card or a piece of paper, write down all the different judgments that your mind has about your teen. Then carry this paper with you in your wallet or purse, and throughout the day, read this list at least three times. Notice any reactions you have. How is it for you to have those thoughts without getting hooked on them? As you know by now, you cannot get rid of those judgment thoughts, but you can learn to have them without acting on them.

Here is a second defusion exercise: throughout the day, check in with yourself about whether the judgment machine is on when you're dealing with your teen or thinking about her. If it is on, then tell yourself *I'm having that thought that…* At the end of the day, write a poem about your judgment machine that includes the criticisms, evaluations, and judgment words that your mind has come up with during the day.

Learning to respond to your thoughts in a different way takes practice, so please be patient with yourself. Practicing will make a difference in your parenting repertoire.

CHAPTER 4

"He Just Shouldn't": When Rules Become Rigid

My country of origin, Bolivia, was under a dictatorship for eight years when I was growing up. From 1970 to 1978, the government prescribed and proscribed the public behaviors of the Bolivian citizens. This is what dictatorships do. Although I do not believe we needed such a rigid set of rules, I do believe that all societies need rules and laws to function; the alternative is complete chaos. In fact, our brains are evolutionarily and biologically conditioned to generate rules that are reinforced by our social environment within different contexts, such as family, school, and friendships. Rules are necessary to function, but taken to an extreme, such as what happens inside a dictatorship—or in a home where rules are rigidly enforced—they can have a devastating effect.

Most parents understandably come up with different rules or expectations about what behaviors are appropriate or not for their children. These rules usually come in the form of *shoulds*, *musts*, or *oughts*, and they usually do their job when your children are young, but everything changes when your child becomes a teenager with a mind of his own. In this chapter, you will look at the rules you make for your teen, the purpose behind them, and how well they are working.

Looking at Your Rules

Maybe you have very few rules, or maybe you have many rules about what's appropriate or inappropriate behavior at home. Every time you are telling your teen he should or shouldn't do something, that's a rule. Sometimes rules or expectations are unspoken, and sometimes they are easier to name. Let's begin by learning about your rules. A clue is to listen to the *should-statements* that you make to yourself and to your teen about your teen's behavior.

EXERCISE: Naming Your Rules

Take out your parenting journal and make a list of all the expectations or rules that you have for your teen. Complete the sentence *My mind says that my teen shouldn't...* and the sentence *My mind says that my teen should...*

When Stefan was asked this question about Benny, his sixteen-year-old son, his responses looked like this:

My mind says that Benny shouldn't...

fight with me when I tell him how to behave.

stay in his room until dinner.

threaten me with suicide.

post any pictures of himself on Facebook.

stay up late playing video games on school days.

spend all his money on iTunes all the time.

My mind says that Benny should...

work during the summer.

do his own laundry.

complete his homework on time.

ask for permission to create accounts on Tumblr or Instagram.

Are these rules similar to the ones you have for your teen? Maybe you have all, some, or none of them. If you carefully observe your teen's behavior in response to your own rules and expectations, what do you notice? Take a couple of moments to reflect on this question, and then write down your answers.

Stefan answered: *No matter how many times I tell him that he can only play video games for one hour at night after doing his homework, he just keeps doing it into the night. Every single night, we have a battle because of this. Sometimes I feel that I come up with a new rule every day because I just don't understand how Benny thinks about the things he does at home.*

Are your rules working? Take a moment to examine which rules are working and which ones aren't.

A teen's noncompliance with the house rules can be a source of problems in your daily family life, and these problems are surely exacerbated when your teen has an emotional switch that goes on too much, too quick, too soon or who simply shuts down when it comes to listening. This is a very sensitive issue for many parents, since part of your job is to create frames of behavior within your family life with the hope that your teen will learn how to behave in different social settings.

It's quite likely that all the rules you have for your teen have an important purpose for you as a parent, which is the only reason you hold on to them. Let's take a minute to look at these rules to fully understand the purpose of holding on to them.

What Is the Purpose Behind Rules?

As our minds come up with evaluations, judgments, and criticisms, they also come up with expectations or rules to organize our internal and external psychological landscapes. The parenting rules you have about your teen's behavior are influenced by many variables, such as your teen's past behaviors, personal family history, and your own upbringing, to name a few.

You, like most parents I work with, probably have good reasons to hold on to different rules when it comes to your teen's behavior, and usually behind each rule, there is a teaching purpose driving it. For instance, Stefan had the rule "no food is allowed in the bedroom" because for him it was important to teach Benny cleanliness and to prepare him for when he goes to college and has to share a room. Other parents mention other principles, such as protecting their teens from being hurt, teaching them how to be more independent, preparing them for the difficult moments in life, or teaching them a sense of accountability. These are all explanations for having different rules.

EXERCISE: What's the Teaching Purpose Behind Your Rules?

Copy this chart into your parenting journal. In the column on the left, list some different rules or expectations you have for your teen. Look carefully at each rule or expectation and see if you recognize a teaching purpose, a reason behind or explanation for it. Write your teaching purpose down next to the rule or expectation that it explains.

Rules or expectations	Teaching purpose or reason

Your teaching purpose may vary or be the same in different cases. Look over this list and then ask yourself, which is more important, the rules or their teaching purpose?

Exercising a teaching purpose is certainly an important part of your parenting job: how else can you help your teen be the best person he can be if it's not by creating limits and a framework for his behavior? Having teaching purposes and rules for your teen's behavior is necessary, understandable, and a reasonable behavior for you or any parent raising a teen. So far, so good, right? However, as with many things in life, applying these rules isn't always easy.

When Rules Are Too Rigid

Over the years working with parents, I have witnessed certain challenges that come up when parents get rigidly fused with specific rules. Here are the most common rules I found parents get hooked on:

My teen should follow the house rules at all times. The wording may vary, but the idea here is that the teen is expected to comply with all rules 24/7. Even if your rules are based on important life principles, and you do your best to put them into practice, rules are likely to get broken at times. Let's be real: most teens cannot comply with a rule longer than a week without breaking it, because that's the nature of being a teen.

I was raised this way, and my teen should be raised the same way. Stefan was holding on to the rules that Benny "shouldn't be fighting with me when I tell him how to behave" and "shouldn't stay in his room until dinner" because that's how he was raised. Stefan struggled to recognize that typical adolescent behavior these days is staying in your bedroom, keeping a messy bedroom, avoiding family gatherings, experimenting sexually, disagreeing with your parents, trying drugs, and even refusing to go to school. Okay, how difficult was it just now to read about typical adolescent behavior? Some parents I work with disagree with me about those behaviors, and I totally get it. The challenge for today's parents is that all those behaviors have become the norm for teens. I'm not saying that it's right that your teen does all those things. The key question here is whether getting fused with the rule *My teen should be raised as I was* helps you respond effectively to your teen's behavior given its social context.

Making sure my teen follows this rule is the only way I can protect him from bad things happening. While most parents want to protect their children, holding tightly to the rule of "not permitting the teen to message people on Facebook without asking me first" becomes a restrictive way of living for today's teen. These days, all teens are texting masters and use texting as their primary form of communication, yet some parents fear that by relaxing such a rule, they are abandoning the principle of protecting their children and are failing at their parenting job. They forget that there may be other things they can do to protect them, such as teaching their teen how to recognize dangerous situations when going out, ask for help when feeling unsafe, or distinguish which Facebook profile is age-appropriate for them, to name a few.

If you're hooked on any of the rules mentioned above, you may be carrying a dictator within your mind, where the rules are too rigid. Let's take a look at how carrying this dictator is working for you and the relationship with your teen.

Where Does the Dictator Within Your Mind Take You?

Parents of teens struggling with intense emotions are often faced with an abundance of situations in which the teen breaks a single house rule or all of them at once. Naturally, the more this happens, the more the dictator within the parent's mind is likely to be turned on. When you're totally hooked on a rule, you may react to it being broken as if your teen had pressed a personal hot button, and you may respond with a laundry list of additional rules.

Within ACT, a fundamental skill is to check in with yourself about whether a particular behavior is working or not in your parenting life. If you determine that it's not working, then you have an opportunity to change it.

EXERCISE: Are Your Rules Working?

Pick up your parenting journal and answer the following questions:

1. What do you do when your teen breaks the rules or fails your expectations?

2. Does your response help your relationship with your teen in the short term?

3. Does your response help in the long term?

If your response to rules being broken hurts your relationship, then it may be that you are fused to a rule that is not working. When Stefan answered these questions, he realized that when he gets fused with the expectation that *Benny should follow rules at all times*, he usually screams at him, throws a series of punishments at him, or comes up with additional rules. In the short term, Benny usually screams back and runs to his bedroom, and then he avoids his father for a couple of days. Stefan continues to feel angry for hours and, in the long term, feels more frustrated and disconnected from Benny.

Looking back at your answers to the questions, can you relate to Stefan's situation?

Getting fused with rules and acting quickly on them is depriving yourself of a chance to choose your response and teach your teen how to handle a difficult situation without hurting the relationship with him. Every time your teen receives a rule about how to behave, he is naturally going to reflect on it, make sense of it from his own perspective, and then figure out whether or not to follow it. And of course, sometimes your teen will simply reject it out of a belief that it's not right for him. That's typical teen behavior. Teens are in the process of learning about themselves, the world, life, and others through their own lenses, not yours.

When the dictator gets activated in your mind, it's as if your only option were to hold on to your rules, which means you're not acknowledging what's going on for your teen, his social context,

41

developmental stage, and unique thought processes. This may even lead you to prescribe more rules. This type of parenting is called an *authoritarian parenting style*. What's the outcome of this style of parenting? It's quite likely that he will continue to reject your rules over and over again. The final outcome of parents insisting on 100 percent compliance with their rules is that they will have a very rocky relationship with their teen; an authoritarian parenting style is simply a recipe for disconnection and isolation between parents and teens.

I'm not saying that having expectations or making rules is a negative thing in and of itself. Rules are necessary for any teen; however, you need to take into consideration the social context of the teen's reality and developmental stage. Adolescence by nature is a time of changes, challenges, and unpredictability. Teens are often moody, argumentative, and opinionated. They tend to like to be alone in their bedroom, are passionate for social media, and sleep long hours. Getting fused to a rule that your teen "should not spend time alone in his bedroom" or "should not do any texting for one month" is not taking into consideration your teen's reality.

Adolescence as a developmental period is intensified when a teen struggles with emotion dysregulation, because he is predisposed to experience higher levels of sensitivity to his environment, heightened emotional experiences, and it takes him longer than it might take someone else to get back to his emotional baseline when upset. A teen once told me, "It's as if suddenly I become a bull and see red all around me. I don't know how to stop it; it's so real."

The only situations in which strict rules apply are when a teen is unsafe because of intentional suicidal plans or impulsive risk-taking behavior.

Summary

Creating expectations and rules for a teen is another parenting task, a natural one. The challenge is when you get fused with your expectations and rules; the dictator within your mind starts prescribing and proscribing your teen's behavior, and then you quickly act on whatever it dictates without pausing to check whether your response is helpful or not in that particular situation. To keep the dictator within your mind in check, it is important for you to do the following:

Watch if the dictator within your mind prescribes rules that ignore your teen's social context, developmental stage, and unique emotional sensitivities. Pay attention to *should*, *must*, or *ought-to* statements. They are cues that the dictator within your mind is on. Keeping the dictator within your mind in check will help you to find workable responses when dealing with your highly sensitive teen. It's doable!

Weekly Practice: Toppling the Dictator

Here is another classic defusion exercise to let your thoughts come and go when the dictator in your mind takes over.

Bring into your mind a moment in which your teen broke a rule, and see if you can catch when the dictator within your mind gets activated. If the answer is yes, give the dictator a name (any name you like). Then, imagine that you're driving on the freeway, bring into your mind all those rules you have for your teen, and place each one of them on a billboard, so you can see the types of fonts, colors, and sizes of each rule as you drive by and they are out of your sight.

CHAPTER 5

"My Time-Traveling Machine": Worries and Ruminations

Tiffany and Ken walk into my therapy office. After we exchange greetings, Ken quickly says, "Don't ask us anything about the weekend. We tried to remind Mariah to ask for time out if she needed it, but nothing mattered to her; she completely ignored us. I tried to talk to her in different ways, but I got no response. Nothing is going to work, she won't do anything we discuss in therapy, and she just won't get better. There is no point in trying; this is how it's always going to be: us trying and her ignoring us. I can totally see what her future will be." His gaze falls to the floor, and it's as though he were no longer present in the room with us.

They come back the following week. While discussing and reviewing empathy skills, Tiffany's voice softens up and she says, "I just don't see the point of practicing empathy skills. I already tried this before. I really try to understand her every day, and guess what? I get yelled at. Why should I do it again?" Tiffany sighs deeply after making this statement.

Have you had moments like this when dealing with your teen? Times in which you certainly did your best to connect with her, address her behavior, parent her the best you could, only to have things go south? You may have noticed that Ken, without realizing it, had thoughts about what the future was going to be like for Mariah, such as *Nothing is going to work; she just won't get better.* Tiffany, on the other hand, had several thoughts about how hard she has tried in the past and how nothing has worked. For both of them, their thoughts, either about the future or about the past, were activated by their attempts to parent Mariah, and they both got stuck on those thoughts; the outcome of acting on those thoughts was to stop trying. Both Ken and Mariah gave up on their parenting task. Is this something you go through? Does your mind ever say things like this about your teen? Let's take a look at your personal time machine.

Your Time Machine

There are so many movies, books, poems, and stories about the past and the future, it raises the question of whether our current interest in the past and the future is any different from what it was histori- cally. Evolution answers this question for us: from hunter-gatherer societies to today, humans have always been interested in the past and the future because of survival; our ancestors had to cultivate the ability to anticipate what could go wrong and what went wrong because of ongoing sources of danger: poor weather conditions, predators, or ongoing hostility with other groups. If our ancestors hadn't developed the ability to go back and forth between the past and the future, they wouldn't have survived. As a result of this evo- lutionary process, our modern minds are hardwired to carry a time machine that naturally switches between the past and the future as a survival mechanism, even though we don't live in prehistorical conditions anymore.

Going back to Ken and Tiffany's situation, it's understandable that Ken's mind began to predict Mariah's future while Tiffany's mind began to recall past similar situations; they both saw the situ- ation of addressing Mariah's behavior as a problem, their minds said *danger*, and quickly their mental time machine got activated. They both were caught on those past and future thoughts and behaved accordingly; they both got fused with their mind-talk.

Should we take a look at how often or not your own time machine gets activated? Let me walk you through an ACT exercise developed by Strosahl, Robinson, and Gustavsson (2012); this activ- ity is very simple and will take up very little of your time.

EXERCISE: Your Time Machine

Read the following paragraph of instructions before you start.

Sit in a comfortable position, and then set a timer for one minute. While sitting, pay attention to what's going on in your mind by noticing whether you're having thoughts about the past, the present, or the future. If you find yourself having a thought or image about the past, label it as "past," if you have a thought or image about the future, label it as "future," and if it's a thought about the present, label it as "present." This may seem like a very silly exercise, but let's see what happens within your mind with this experiment. Do your best to label every thought and image that shows up in your mind for the next minute. When the timer goes off, notice whether your mind came up with more thoughts about the past, present, or future.

Every time you do this exercise, the outcome could be different based on your time-machine activity, but most often our mind quickly travels to the past or future and rarely stays in the present.

If we don't pay attention and choose our response, we can easily get hooked on those time-traveling thoughts, ignore the present in a fraction of seconds, and reactively act on past or future thoughts. Distinguishing when your time machine turns on and whether it is bringing in past or future thoughts is another important skill in your parenting repertoire, because the more you get hooked on those thoughts, the less present you are with your teen and the fewer chances you have to choose an effective parenting response in the moment.

Chewing on Your Thoughts

When the time machine gets activated, we spend a lot of time going over and over things about the past or about possible future situations. Like cows, we chew and chew, but instead of chewing grass, we chew our thoughts over and over; we dwell on them. Dwelling on potential future scenarios or what might happen is called *worry;*

dwelling on the past as if we were continually replaying over and over an old CD is called *rumination*. Worry and rumination have one thing in common: they are hijackers of the present moment, and because of evolution, we naturally struggle being in the present and have the tendency to go back and forth between the past and the future as a way to avoid potential future problems. Our mind, as usual, is just doing its job: protecting us from bad things happening. The question is whether the time machine works for you or against you. Do worry and rumination help the relationship with your teen or make things harder for the two of you?

If you recall, Tiffany and Ken's time machines took their minds into different places, they ended up behaving based on those thoughts, but the outcome was the same: they both got fused with worry thoughts and ruminative thoughts and ended up being pulled away from what was most important to them—addressing Mariah's behavior in the present—as if they were prisoners of their time machines.

EXERCISE: When Your Time Machine Is On

Let's take a look at what you go through when your time machine gets activated and you get fused with those time-traveling thoughts. Pick up your parenting journal and recall a memory with your teen when your time machine turned on and you got hooked on ruminative or worry thoughts. Briefly describe the situation, how you behaved in that particular moment, and whether your parenting behavior was helpful or not for the relationship with your teen. If your behavior helped you be the parent you want to be for your teen, kudos to you; if it wasn't helpful, write down what you could have done differently.

When he did this exercise, Ken identified another moment when his time machine got activated when dealing with Mariah: he recalled a conversation when Mariah requested time alone in her bedroom. Kevin's time machine came up with the following thoughts: *Over the last six months, when she goes to her bedroom, she gets depressed, tearful, and really disconnected from us; then she drinks, cuts, or starts posting stuff on Facebook.* With his time machine turned on, Ken quickly and firmly responded to Mariah: "You're forbidden to be in your bedroom alone. That's not happening. Staying by yourself in your bedroom is not an option anymore."

When Ken reflected on whether that response was helpful or not when dealing with Mariah's request in that moment, he acknowledged that his time machine took him into past thoughts and he responded automatically. He didn't give himself a chance to pause and come up with a different response, such as "I understand you would like to be alone in your bedroom, I get that it's important to you to spend time alone in your bedroom, but it's worrisome to me because of what has happened in the past with cutting, drinking, and posting on Facebook. I care for you, and I understand your need for alone time, but we have to come up with a plan together, so I can make sure you're safe on your own in your bedroom."

Moving forward, and as a general principle when dealing with your teen, when your time machine turns on, make sure to check whether or not you get fused with those sticky past or future thoughts, and then check whether your parenting response is going to be helpful or not in that precise moment.

The more you notice and practice defusion to unhook from these tricky time-traveling thoughts, the better it will get for you; soon it will feel natural for you to pause in the moment, recognize those past or future thoughts, see more clearly what a helpful response could be, and choose your parenting behavior. This takes practice, and even if things don't go perfectly, and at times you get fused with future or past thoughts, as long as you notice what's going on with your parenting mind as you go about your daily life, it will just get better.

Keep it up and don't let your mind play tricks on you. Your teen needs you in this moment, and there is no one better than you to teach her how to handle tough times.

When the Time Machine Works Well

I am not saying that every time you start thinking about the past or future is necessarily wrong or unhelpful. There have been times when thinking about the past has allowed me to learn a great deal about myself, and thinking about the future has allowed me to come up with future projects, such as writing this book. All I'm suggesting is that it is very important to distinguish when worry and rumination are preventing you from doing what's important to you as a parent. In the case of Ken and Tiffany, they really wanted to address Mariah's behavior, but when they got fused with their thoughts, they dropped the ball on parenting their daughter. It's also completely understandable that as you are parenting a teen who struggles with intense emotions, you might be more apt to ruminate about the past or be on edge about the future regarding your teen, especially when you are in the midst of upsetting situations with her.

Going back and forth between the present and the past or the future is a natural mind activity; your mind, and everyone else's mind, does it. There is nothing wrong with this back-and-forth by itself; the challenge is when these cousin-thoughts drive unhelpful parenting behaviors, interfering with your ability to parent, and at the end worsen a situation with your highly sensitive teen.

Your mind is just doing its job: generating all types of past and future scenarios, and it will always do so because of the years of training it has had throughout human history. But at the end, you can choose your parenting behavior.

Summary

Again, looking into the past can be very helpful because we can learn about ourselves, others, and our successes and mistakes. Thinking about the future can allow us to plan projects, come up with new dreams, and see new horizons in our lives. However, if you find yourself dwelling repeatedly on thoughts or images about a particular past moment or about the future, to the point that you're worrying or ruminating, then you're being hijacked away from the present moment, and your time-traveling thoughts have taken charge.

If you do not pay attention and you fail to distinguish these moments, your parenting behavior can be compromised. The past cannot be changed and the future cannot be predicted; all you have is the moment to choose your parenting response. Learning to check in with yourself, whether your mind takes you into the past or the future, is a key skill that will allow you to defuse from troublesome thoughts and to choose your parenting response.

Weekly Practice: Staying in the Present

Slowing down and staying in the present are difficult tasks for any parents, since more often than not you may have multiple errands to run at once, such as picking up your teen from school, getting groceries or art supplies, going to soccer practice, and so on. Undoubtedly, you're facing multiple demands for your time and attention. Here are a couple of exercises to try this week to help you stay in the present.

Set three reminders either on your cell phone or on your watch as cues to check in with yourself as to whether your time machine is active or not in that moment. Ask yourself whether you're in the present, the past, or the future.

Find a comfortable position, and for a couple moments close your eyes. Then, after taking a few slow breaths, imagine that you're sitting on a bench next to a stream of water that keeps running and carries leaves along. Every time your mind comes up with a past or future thought, place it on a leaf and let it float on by until it is out of sight. If your mind comes up with any thoughts about this exercise, gently place that thought onto a leaf as well and let it float by.

CHAPTER 6

"I Suck as a Parent": Mind Stories

Did you ever watch a movie or read a book that you were so into that you couldn't stop talking and thinking about it? A story can totally absorb us anytime, anywhere. In the next pages, you will discover some of the stories you have about your teen and yourself as a parent and how they impact your parenting life. Are you ready to start?

Once Upon a Time...

A couple of years ago, I received an e-mail from a parent, Stacey, who wrote, "I just opened Mark's backpack and found new cutting gear, two packs of Marlboros, one opened, and his wallet with $50. I don't know where that money is coming from...this is very disheartening to me, because my husband and I have talked to him multiple times. We have encouraged him to trust us, to tell us what's going on, and he keeps rejecting any help we offer him. I honestly don't know what else to do. I feel I have failed as a mother. I have managed so many difficult situations in my life successfully, but I can't seem to help my own son. It seems I'm doing a poor job as a mother. It just seems I suck as a parent...and the truth is that I have been feeling like this for a long time now."

Other times, Stacey has come to parent coaching sessions with other narratives: "I can't take his disrespect anymore. Mark has become a verbally abusive teen, tells me anything he wants, he thinks he can get anything he wants, and that's just not right. I'm going to take away all his electronic devices, and he can throw a tantrum if he wants or even move out, but all of this disrespect needs to stop right away. I have spent tons of money on helping him to get better, but he doesn't want to get better, and until he changes his mind, I'm not going to support his vices."

When Stacey fuses with the thought *I am a failure as a mother*, she usually disengages from parenting her son Mark, avoids saying no to him, and gives in to any request he has, whether it's going out with friends, borrowing the car, or asking for money. On the other hand, when she fuses with the thought *Mark is disrespectful*, she adopts an authoritarian parenting behavior, disregards any potential explanation he may have, and acts as if doesn't care for him.

In both situations, Stacey is hooked on a narrative, a story, about who she is and who Mark is. Let's go a little bit more into these *mind stories*.

Our Master Author

Our mind is a very active organ and has an incredible capacity to quickly come up with thoughts, images, hypotheses, fantasies, theories, cause-effect relationships, work projects, opinions, and narratives about all types of subjects, including ourselves and the people around us. Stories or narratives are one of these mind creations; when I use the term *stories* or *narratives*, I'm simply referring to a string of words, sentences, or paragraphs put together. Some of these stories are new, fun, and interesting, and others are old, harsh, and painful, and have been spinning over and over in our mind since we were young.

Has it ever happened to you that while you were driving, you were so trapped by a story in your mind that, without realizing it, you got lost and didn't know when you took the wrong exit? Or have you ever been in a conversation with a friend or a significant other and, without realizing that your mind had taken you into a gripping story, the next thing you knew, you hadn't heard a word of what the other person was saying? There are many examples of how we get caught up in a story as if we carried a master author within us. And guess what? No one is exempt from having that capacity: as long as we're alive, the master author within our mind will continuously create stories about ourselves, others, and any other theme.

EXERCISE: What Are Your Stories?

Here is an exercise for you to check out some of the stories that your mind may have naturally come up with over the years about you and your teen. Pick up your parenting journal and complete the following sentences with the first narrative that comes to mind:

My story telling mind says that:

When I was a kid, I was... because...

When I was a teenager, I was... because...

When I was in my twenties, I was... because...

Now I'm... because...

My teen is... because...

When my teen was a toddler, he was... because...

Now my teen is... because...

As a parent, I'm... because...

What did you come up with? Were there any similarities in these stories? Any differences? Any themes you may have noticed?

When I do this exercise with my clients, I often hear, "But those stories are true! All those stories about myself and my teen are true." If you have a similar response, let me remind you that our minds naturally come up with thousands of narratives; some of them are certainly true, but that doesn't mean that all of them are accurate. More often than not, the stories we have are far from being the truth. Imagine if all the thoughts, memories, or images that showed up in your mind throughout the day were real? Would that even be possible? Not really.

Don't take my word for this. Just pay attention to your mind throughout the day and see what happens. By the end of the day, if you really paid attention, you would notice all types of narrations that went through your mind, sensical and nonsensical ones, to the point that you may have even thought about firing your mind or giving it a minivacation.

Our mind never shuts up, it never gets quiet, it's ceaselessly generating content. A key question to ask when getting caught in a mind story, or any sticky thoughts or narratives, is not whether the story is accurate or not, true or not, but whether it's helpful or not at a given moment in our life. There is a time and place for getting hooked on your mind stories: when you're planning a trip, thinking about a new project for the house, or watching a film, for example; in those moments, getting fused with your mind stories can drive very effective behavior in the moment. Here is a different scenario: how many hours do you spend at night going over stories of sadness, frustration, worry, blame, or anger about your teen or yourself? Is getting hooked on those stories helpful to you at those particular times? Maybe not.

If you hold rigidly to those mind stories about yourself or your teen, they become like a filter through which you see everything; eventually, you will not be able to see your teen for who he is or yourself for who you are as a parent. This is especially complicated when parenting a teen who struggles with emotion dysregulation problems since, more often than not, you have to deal with ongoing fights, arguments, and erratic behaviors, to name a few challenging situations. Getting fused onto mind stories in moments of high emotionality makes things very challenging for you and your teen; this is because mind narratives can be so persuasive that you won't even listen to your teen, since your mind is simply adding data to the "truth" about who your teen is, and you will quickly lose your ability to distinguish your mind narrative from your teen's behavior even though they can be very different. Finally, you end up taking steps that are far from handling the situation effectively.

In Stacey's case, when she gets fused with and behaves according to her *failure* story, she disengages from parenting Mark, and when she believes the mind story of Mark being *disrespectful at all times*, she assumes an authoritarian parenting style, which increases conflict with him.

Keep in mind that your teen will remember you as a parent based on what you did, not on what you felt, thought, or imagined doing. Getting fused with a single narrative that your mind comes up with about your teen will simply make you a prisoner of the story of that moment. What can you do instead of continuing to get fused to your mind stories? Any thoughts? What about…

Getting Unhooked from Your Mind Stories

What about getting unhooked from your mind stories, so you can behave as the parent you want to be and not as the parent that the master author of your mind pushes you to be? If, after reading this last sentence, you're thinking about telling yourself positive stories as a way to counter the negative ones you have about yourself as a parent or your teen, let's take a look into this. Let me walk you through a classic ACT exercise developed by Hayes, Strosahl, and Wilson (2012) and adapted for this book.

EXERCISE: Think About a Chessboard

See if you can find a relaxed position and imagine for a second a chessboard. Imagine that your stories, narratives, or tales about who you are as a parent are like pieces on a chessboard; sometimes, your mind comes up with negative stories you dislike about who you are as a parent, and then, naturally your mind comes up with positive tales about who you are as a parent as a way of countering the adverse ones. And as in chess, the pieces make moves and fight against each other, as your positive and negative stories do at times, pulling you forward and backward across the board. Sometimes, you get hooked on the positive ones; sometimes you get hooked on the negative ones.

Now imagine for a second that you're the chessboard itself, and instead of getting hooked on the chess battle between your positive and negative narratives, you just watch them. You just observe them as they play out their game; you just have them.

Any reactions to this exercise? Can you notice the difference between being hooked on positive and negative stories about yourself and just having these stories without acting on them? Although a counterargument approach was very popular in pop psychology, research over the last decade has consistently shown us that countering or arguing against our negative narratives actually reinforces them and increases their frequency. As long as we're alive, our master author will come up with all types of elaborate narratives about all types of situations, objects, people, and themes, both positive and negative ones. Mind stories come and go, one after another, and it's hard to keep track of them or fight against them, because they're so many, and guess what? There will be many more mind stories to come and go as long as you're alive.

Are you willing to do something more helpful for the relationship with your teen than getting fused to those mind stories and acting on them? If so, turn on the defusion switch. How? By noticing and naming the story about yourself or your teen. Naming the story is simply giving it a name that helps you to recognize it when it's showing up and to look at it for what it is: a collection of thoughts. When Stacey got introduced to defusion, she named her story as "the sucking story." She also decided to name the story about Mark as "the disrespectful story." Naming is like pressing the brake when driving the car; it invites you to pause. By naming her stories, Stacey was able to pause, breathe, check whether those stories were helpful or not, and choose a response to her son's behavior in the moment, instead of going on automatic pilot mode.

EXERCISE: Name That Story

Grab your parenting journal, look back at your previous entry where you listed what your storytelling mind says about you and your teen, and follow this defusion exercise:

1. Name each story with a different name (such as "my cranky story," "my teen sucks story," "I'm not a good enough parent story").

2. Notice what the story pushes you to do.

3. Take a deep breath.

4. Check in with yourself whether acting on the story would be helpful or not. Is that behavior going to be helpful in that moment and take you closer to being the parent you want to be?

Write down your responses to this defusion exercise and do your best to go back to it when a new narrative shows up in your mind and you're getting hooked on it.

This defusion exercise is going to give you more space to be present with yourself and your teen, so you can choose your parenting behavior. Completing this defusion exercise in your journal at first is a good way to practice this skill; eventually, you want to get to the point where you practice defusion every time a triggering situation shows up and you're getting trapped by a narrative.

Some of the narratives you carry may come along with deep pain, sadness, or disappointment; defusing from the story is not about denying the pain that comes with it but about simply allowing you to be present in the moment instead of having the narrative take over the moment. A former client of mine lost her oldest son in a car accident; her mind came up with the story *I'm not a good mother* because of this experience. Sadly, when talking to her youngest son, the story was so loud that she missed the moment when the little one started calling her Mom or when his hands tried to hold on to her for a couple of moments.

Once again, the master author of your mind will come up with all types of narratives, but you can learn to catch them in action before they hijack you away from the present moment and take away your opportunity to choose your response.

Summary

This chapter was focused on noticing how our minds naturally come with all types of stories or narratives about ourselves, others, and any situation we're exposed to. Our minds, like popcorn machines, are incessantly active and will continue to come up with all types of narratives throughout our life. Is this a problem? You may not like the stories, you may not feel comfortable with them, but having them is not really the problem. The problem is when you get fused with every single narrative you have and act based on these narratives as if they were absolute truths, without checking whether they are helpful or not in that particular moment.

As you have read in earlier chapters, looking at the workability of each type of mind noise (judgments, criticisms, evaluations, narratives, rules, past and future thoughts) is a touchstone within ACT. In your parenting job, you're going to encounter an infinite number of mind stories about your teen and yourself, especially if your teen suffers with emotion dysregulation problems, since his behaviors may be more often erratic than constant. Defusing and defusing again from those mind stories is a key skill for being the parent you want to be, and not what the author mind of your mind pushes you to be, in a given moment. You can choose how to behave; it's doable.

Weekly Practice: Defusing from Your Mind Stories

Here is another defusion exercise. After choosing and naming a mind story about yourself as a parent, imagine you're calling for a taxi cab, and visualize your mind story in the form of a name—a string of words with color, shape, and size—taking the cab, and then see the mind story getting in the cab and leaving.

You can also create your own defusion exercises. For instance, a client of mine imagined the T-shirts of his favorite football players having a slogan based on his story as a parent, "Failure," and then saw the players run onto the field.

For this next defusion exercise, find a comfortable position and give yourself approximately ten minutes to complete it; first read the directions, so you know what to expect, record them at a slow pace, and then listen to them privately.

> For a couple of minutes, see if you can bring your attention
> to your breathing and the qualities of it every time you're

breathing in and breathing out. Gently, allow yourself to be present in this precise moment; see if you can bring into your mind one of those stories you have been carrying about yourself as a parent and, while holding on to it, notice how it feels to have this narrative...see if you can scan your body from head to toe searching for any physical sensation... breathe slowly...see if there is any emotion associated with it...breathe slowly again...see if there are any urges to get rid of this emotion or any other urges to do something about it...breathe slowly again. Gently notice how it is to have the story without becoming the story, see if you can make room for those sensations, emotions, and action urges that come with this narrative...take a deep breath and notice one more time what it feels like for you to have the story without fighting against it, pushing it away, or denying it...but simply having it. Breathe again and after taking three deep breaths, open your eyes and bring yourself back into the room.

CHAPTER 7

"It's an Emotional Rollercoaster": Handling Those Intense Emotions

Jordana sent the following text to her mother, Abby: "My boyfriend is leaving and I don't know what I am going to do. I'm afraid I'm going to cut—not just once but multiple times, and I don't want you to stop me. I'm not ready to give up the only tool that helps me to handle my pain."

Abby, read the text, breathed deeply, and felt a knot in her stomach. A wave of hopelessness washed over her. She breathed again and quickly texted back to Jordana: "It's very selfish of you to tell me you're going to cut now, after all the money I spent in therapy on you; it's not fair and not a smart decision. How come you cannot be the strong kid you were before? I don't understand." While typing that text, her heart was beating fast, her body temperature was rising, and anger started taking over. Abby didn't get any reply from Jordana, even though she was often checking her messages while experiencing ongoing levels of stress. As the afternoon progressed, she started feeling shame for sending her last text to Jordana and then found herself crying about it.

Up to this point, we have focused on different types of thoughts—stories, past and future thoughts, judgments, and rules—that you may struggle with in your parenting role. But other times your experience can be dominated by intense emotions, such as what Abby was feeling upon reading her daughter's text. Just to clarify, the terms *feelings* and *emotions* are used interchangeably in this chapter. When you are parenting a highly sensitive teen, sometimes you know what is likely to set your teen off; other times, you don't know what just happened and are surprised to see your teen's strong reaction. If you pay attention to your own experience, you will discover that at times you go through a similar process, like Abby who experienced a significant amount of hopelessness after receiving a text from her daughter Jordana informing her of her intention to cut.

Noticing the Emotional Rollercoaster

The experience of going through several intense and different emotions is like being on an emotional rollercoaster; you are simply swept up in the emotion with no sense of control over where it's taking you. The emotional experience may be so intense that you cannot imagine another way of behaving except for doing exactly what the emotion pushes you to do. Parenting is a very rewarding task, and simultaneously it is extremely hard; parents of teens suffering with emotional vulnerability often feel stressed out, impatient, angry, frustrated, powerless, or disappointed at their teens' reactivity; all these emotional experiences are completely natural, given that as humans we are wired to experience all of them. As one of my friends said, we are "emotional beings." The tricky part of this emotional reality is that our feelings play tricks on us; if we don't pay attention, we won't even realize we are experiencing them until we just react to them, and then we may be swamped by an even greater sense of sadness, anger, hurt, distrust, resentment, guilt, and shame. It's as if our emotions were dictating everything we do in those moments.

Traditionally, psychological literature distinguished "positive" versus "negative" feelings and encouraged us to do everything possible to experience only positive emotions and to avoid, at all costs, negative emotions. We were taught that if an uncomfortable emotion showed up, we should replace it with a positive one. Within the ACT model, however, we emphasize that all types of emotional reactions are simply emotional reactions, neither good nor bad.

Seeing feelings as good or bad is simply another judgment thought. When we undergo an uncomfortable emotion, we do everything we can to run away from it, to get rid of it. However, the more we try to escape it, the more intense it becomes, because all strategies to suppress it simply magnify it. The more you don't want to feel anxious, the more anxious you're going to feel; the more you don't want to feel stressed, the more stressed you're going to feel. It's far more useful to look at whether our *response* to a given emotion is helpful or not in the situation in which it arises.

When your teen is showing *reactive* behaviors, such as screaming, threatening, or lashing out, any parent will feel challenged, and a natural response is to do everything you can to immediately stop both your teen's behavior and the emotional discomfort you're going through. This is a very common dynamic for parents raising teens with intense emotional sensitivity, so let's take a look at the most difficult emotions you encounter in your parenting job.

EXERCISE: Your Feelings

For a couple of moments, think about a difficult situation you had with your teen this past week. Close your eyes if that helps you remember. Do your best to imagine that particular memory as vividly as possible; notice the specifics of that moment between the two of you, and hold this image in your mind for a couple of minutes. Then do your best to answer the following questions in your parenting journal:

1. Do you notice a particular bodily sensation? Take a couple of minutes to scan your body from head to toe and pay attention to some common areas, such as your tummy, chest, shoulders, throat, or jaws.

2. How intense is this physical experience? Moderately, mildly, or severely intense?

3. Can you name this emotion? You can name the emotion by simply saying *Here is a feeling of...* Naming the emotion like this is very important because telling yourself things like *I'm angry*, or *I'm sad* implies that your personal identity

65

as a whole is defined by the emotion, which magnifies the experience. You're certainly more than the emotion you're working on.

4. Can you notice what this feeling is asking you to do? Do your best to recognize any impulse or urge associated with this emotion. What do you feel like doing? Here is the caveat—it's quite natural that in the process of recognizing these urges you may want to go along with them—but keep in mind that your task here is to simply describe your urges and then go back to focusing on the emotion. This is a fundamental step, to distinguish the difference between *being* the emotion and *having* the emotion. Being the emotion is automatically doing anything the emotion asks you to do, and having the emotion is simply acknowledging its existence.

5. Are you having any thoughts along with this emotion?

6. Can you simply describe those thoughts and images to yourself? You can say something along the lines of, *I'm having the thoughts...*

7. Finally, switch the focus of your attention to your breathing, and slowly notice the quality of every breath as you draw it in and let it out.

After completing this exercise, you may have noticed that emotions have a life of their own, and by simply watching them, without trying to change them, you allow these feelings to follow their natural course.

The better you can handle your emotions, the better you will be able to handle your teen's emotional responses. The starting point is always looking within and recognizing your own uncomfortable feelings to figure out how to respond to them and to your teens' problematic behaviors; without looking inward, you're at the mercy of the emotional rollercoaster.

Now let's take a closer look at the most common strategies parents use when dealing with intense emotions.

Emotion Management Strategies

Parents, like any human beings, rely on all types of strategies to manage their emotions and their parental distress. These strategies take different forms, but all have a single purpose: to control your emotional struggle and avoid discomfort at all costs.

It's useful to treat these go-to emotion management strategies in a lighthearted manner rather than judge them, because at the end, you're doing the best you can raising your dysregulated teen. Notice if one or more of these strategies applies to you.

The Disconnector

If you're using the disconnector emotion management strategy, it's quite likely that when having an intense feeling, you leave the situation, either physically or emotionally, that is triggering it. For instance, when his daughter questioned him about the T-shirt he gave her for her birthday, George felt so hurt that without saying anything, he simply left his daughter in the living room and walked toward the backyard. He had to physically remove himself from that painful experience.

The Pusher

When your feelings are very strong, you try to push them away immediately using different substances, such as alcohol, food, or even prescription medications; you take these substances to tamp down the intense emotional reactions you are having. One of my clients said, "I better visit Xanax nation when dealing with my teen this afternoon because it's going to be a rough conversation."

The Distracter

If you use the distracter strategy, you will use any activity to distract yourself from the uncomfortable emotions you experience when dealing with your teen. For instance, Claire tends to spend hours watching television, working at the office, surfing the Internet, or doing online gambling to distract herself from the pain of learning her daughter has been cutting over the last six months.

The Externalizer

Using the externalizer strategy means that you explain your intense emotions by looking at your teen's behaviors as the only cause of them. Focusing exclusively on your teen's behavior or blaming her for how you feel is an indication that you are not looking at your own emotional experience and how that experience is driving your parenting behavior in a given moment.

The Surrenderer

If you "give in" to whatever the emotion tells you to do, you are relying on a surrender type of emotion management strategy. For instance, if you feel powerless, you may simply give in and go along with whatever your teen requests, says, or does. Or if you're feeling angry, you simply act on that anger and perhaps scream at your teen, lash out, and even called her names. In both examples, you go along with the emotion without looking at the consequences of your parenting responses for you, your teen, or the relationship between the two of you. It's as if you were reactively going with the flow of emotions, jumping from one point of the emotional chain to another point.

These emotion management strategies may be helpful at times. For instance, if you're getting angry and you catch yourself getting ready to scream at your need, it's more helpful to use a disconnector strategy than to act on anger. However, it's a much different scenario if you rely on these strategies as a default mode when experiencing high emotionality and without looking at whether they're improving or worsening the challenging moments you go through with your teen.

When using these strategies rigidly, they quickly transform into *control and avoidance strategies* that get activated at the maximum level any time you experience parental distress; they help you perform an escapist act the moment an uncomfortable emotion appears, and in the short term, they work. However, the consequence of rigidly using these strategies is that the emotions you are escaping from will not only reappear but also revisit you with more intensity.

The more you engage in an escapist act, it's like the more you're feeding a little tiger with a piece of steak; at some point the little tiger gets bigger, and instead of being satisfied with a single piece of steak, it will demand more pieces. Similarly, the uncomfortable emotion you're trying to escape from, instead of pushing you to escape from a single uncomfortable situation, will demand you escape from all situations that trigger it; then the emotional rollercoaster has simply taken over and you lose the option to choose your parenting response.

Summary

The emotional rollercoaster will continue happening until you learn to handle all the uncomfortable emotions associated with parental distress without running away from them. Learning to notice your emotional experience and recognizing the different emotional strategies you use—pusher, disconnector, externalizer, surrenderer, distracter—are the first steps to choose your behavioral response when dealing with your highly sensitive teen.

Weekly Practice: Playing Emotion Detective

For the next couple of days, especially when feeling triggered by your teen's behavior, see if you can carefully notice, as an emotion detective, the most intense emotion that you experience, the physical experience of it, the intensity of it, your go-to emotion management strategy, and finally, any impulses to act on it.

CHAPTER 8

"What Type of Parent Do I Want to Be?": Your Parenting Values

It's time to open the door to an area that is unique and key to ACT: your parenting values. As mentioned in chapter 1, traditional parenting classes or even self-help books often ask you to identify your goals. Often these goals are to make concrete changes in your teen's behavior, making sure your teen cleans his bedroom every weekend or stopping him from screaming, to name a couple of examples. While establishing goals may look initially useful, an exclusive focus on them won't improve the relationship with your highly sensitive teen, and these goals all fall short in helping you to keep the larger picture of your parenting role.

ACT takes parenting to a very different level by asking: *Who do you want to be as a parent, and what's really important to you?* Do you remember the last time you asked yourself this question: *What type of parent do I want to be?* Parenting a teen with intense emotional vulnerabilities is challenging, and parents usually don't have a chance to pause and figure out what really drives them as parents. Do you relate to that? Parenting becomes another task you perform as you go throughout the day, like piloting a ship on a vast ocean without a compass.

Parenting values are like the compass for the ship; they're qualities that you want to be remembered for by your teen; they give you a sense of purpose and direction; they are chosen ways of being as a parent. And fundamentally, they make your parenting job worth living.

Clarifying Your Parenting Values

Before you start, let's distinguish what parenting values are and what they are not, and let's take a look at a few misconceptions about them.

Values Are Not Goals

This is a very important distinction, since most people frantically come up with a laundry list of actions to take, which may look good on paper but don't necessarily add meaning, fulfillment, and direction to their lives. Goals are specific actions or behaviors you take to move toward your values, your chosen destination. For instance, being married is not a value but a goal toward becoming the partner you want to be in a relationship; getting pregnant is a goal or a step toward becoming a loving mother. There is a large difference between doing things "just because" and doing things because they matter to you.

EXERCISE: Distinguishing Values from Goals

Here is a mini exercise for you to distinguish values from goals. After reading the items on the list below, see if you can determine whether the item is a value or a goal:

- Attending your son's graduation

- Being active

- Texting your son

- Making a meal for your son

- Being caring

- Giving a stipend to your son

- Teaching responsibility to your son

The only three values in the list above are "being caring," "being active," and "teaching responsibility to your son." Again, goals help you move toward your values, your destination.

Values Are Not Morals

Choosing your values has nothing to do with religious or spiritual beliefs, societal rules, or legal codes of conduct. Within ACT, your parenting values are chosen qualities of being what you want to stand up for as a parent and are personal only to you.

Values Are Not Wishes or Wants

Values are not the same as wants, needs, and desires about your teen's behavior. For example, *I want my teen to be more appreciative of all the money I'm spending on him* is clearly a wish. Although it's understandable that parents want to feel appreciated for what they do for their teens, wishing a teen to behave in one way or another is not a value; it's a wishful thought. Wanting to be treated by your teen in a certain way is a want.

Values Are Not Feelings

Sometimes when initiating a conversation about values with the parents I work with, I hear them saying things like, "I really value feeling good about the relationship with my teen. That's important to me." The challenge with this statement is that values are not feelings and you don't have control over how you feel in a given moment; feelings come and go like waves in the ocean. You, I, and everyone around us are wired to experience a full range of emotions—that's our natural makeup—but experiencing one feeling versus another does not mean you're living your values; you're just feeling.

Now that you know what values are and are not, let's figure out what really matters to you as a parent, shall we? Being clear about your parenting values will allow you to be clear about how to respond to parenting in general and, in particular, to those rocky moments when dealing with your highly sensitive teen. For instance, your parenting values will help you to decide whether to scream back at your teen when he's yelling or to verbally appreciate his struggle; or whether you work longer hours for more money or you spend extra time with your teen even though you make less money.

Here is an exercise that will help you reflect on what is really important to you as a parent; make sure you have your parenting journal next to you, so you can jot down your responses after completing this exercise.

EXERCISE: Your Final Days on Earth

Read the directions below slowly and see what you come up with at the end of it.

Imagine you have lived your life the best you could up to this point. Some things went as you wanted them to go, some things were difficult, but here you are today. You have had to face ongoing difficulties with your dysregulated teen, and you have certainly done your best to manage this struggle. You have tried talking to him, talking to others, medication, therapy, you name it, but the outcome has remained the same. Things with your teen are how they are right now. You didn't plan for it; it just happened. However, things take a new course for you in this moment, and you're notified that you're going to die. Read that last sentence again, and confirm what it says: You're going to die within the next twenty-four hours. Suddenly you start breathing fast and realize you only have a short amount of time to be alive and prepare for your final departure. You are also invited to ask yourself this question: *Given how things are with my teen right now, what type of parent do I want to be?* You're living your last day on earth. You're running out of time. There is no turning back. This is it. Please reflect on this, and instead of rushing to answer, breathe, and look again inside for your response.

Write down what you came up with at the end of this exercise, and see if you can identify your parenting values. Values are usually stated with verbs because they show ongoing continuity for the parent you want to be: for example, a parenting value is being loving, or teaching responsibility.

After completing the exercise, Marcia stated that raising her teen has been a beautiful journey and also a scary one because she became a mother when she was twenty-one years old and didn't know what it meant to raise a kid at that time. Over the years, she did her best when her teen's emotional switch went on and off, sometimes daily, other times sporadically. Moving forward, Marcia wants to be an "accepting mother."

Here is another exercise for you to identify your parenting values while reflecting on different moments in your parenting. This exercise was adapted from the Sweet Spot exercise (Wilson 2008). You're advised to find a comfortable position for yourself to get the most out of it. I suggest you read the script below slowly, record it on your cell phone or another recording device, and then listen to it.

EXERCISE: Pure Moments of Purpose

Take a couple of moments to get comfortable where you're sitting or standing, and if necessary, make any adjustments to your posture, so you can be at ease. If possible, allow your eyes to close and slowly start focusing on your breathing. Notice the pace, rhythm, and movement of breathing in and breathing out. Allow yourself to be present with your breathing as it comes and goes for a couple of moments. If you find yourself getting distracted from your breathing, very gently bring your attention back to every moment you inhale and exhale. Notice the quality of your breathing as it is. Are you breathing fast? Are you breathing slowly? Notice the movement of breathing. Can you track the movement of the air that goes through your nostrils and moves through your body? Slowly and with intention allow yourself to simply notice this very important function of your body, your breathing.

We are going to switch gears now and for the next couple of moments you're invited to bring into your mind a particular memory of your teen when he was a baby and you found purpose in your parenting job. It's a moment in which you were the parent you wanted to be; it's a perfect moment between the two of you. Allow yourself to notice the experience of holding this memory and gently notice how it feels in your body. Notice any physical reaction, any emotion that comes to you, any thoughts related to it. Allow yourself to be fully present with this memory of pure connection.

With gentleness, let this image of having purpose with your baby fade from your mind and go back to paying attention to your breathing. Notice again the quality of your breathing: every time you inhale and exhale. Bring your attention back to this very basic and powerful function of your body by noticing the subtleties of it, breath by breath. Notice the temperature of the air when you inhale and exhale, the pace of your breathing, and simply notice the flow of your breath as it enters and leaves your body.

As you breathe in and breathe out, bring to your mind an image of another moment of a time in which you found purpose as a parent with your teen when he was a child. It doesn't need to be a major event, but simply one of those moments between the two of you in which you're fully present with him—a moment in which you experience the preciousness of being a parent. Do the best you can to bring that image to mind as vividly as possible. Notice the colors, sounds, and even smells of that unique moment and gently hold it in your mind for a couple of moments. There is no need to rush, no need to do anything but hold this image with a sense of being open to it and appreciating the moment. It's a moment of connection. It's an invitation for you to get in contact with the parent you were in that precise moment with your kid. As you did with the first image, allow yourself to notice the experience of holding this moment of connection and gently notice how it feels in your body. Notice any emotion you're experiencing or any sensation you may be experiencing; you can also notice if there are any thoughts related to that particular memory. Once again, the invitation is for you to allow yourself to be fully present with this moment of connection.

Slowly and with intention, let this image fade from your mind and return your attention to your breathing. Now slowly turn your attention to your breathing as you breathe in and out. Bring awareness to the qualities of your breath going in and out of your body. Notice the subtle sensations of breathing in your body. Allow yourself to be present with the flow of your breath.

And for last time, let go of paying attention to your breathing and imagine a moment you had with your teen as a teenager. Imagine a moment in which you find your direction as a parent. As you did with the other two images, bring to your mind this very special moment between the two of you, and with intention, notice this moment for what it is. See if you can let go of trying to understand this moment of fulfillment with words. See if you can simply let it be what it is, a moment of finding purpose in your parenting job, and fully immerse yourself in it by simply being present with it. Notice the qualities of the moment, any feelings that come to you, any sensations, and then gently focus on what it feels like, inhale, exhale slowly, and then completely let go of all these images as well as the exercise. Take three deep, slow breaths before transitioning out of this exercise. Open your eyes, and slowly return your attention back to the room around you.

Take out your parenting journal and write down the different reactions you had to the three images of those moments of experiencing purpose in your role as parent when he was a baby, a child, and then a teen. After writing, read your responses to each one of these images and see if you can identify any important quality of parenting that may have been revealed to you. Is there a parenting value there for you? Is there more than one parenting value that is important to you?

When Wanda completed this values exercise, she paused, and after a long breath, she said, "I forgot how important it is for me to be a trustworthy parent for my teen."

Now that you have clarified your values, let's move on to another important ACT skill: living your values. Remember that, like a compass, your chosen parenting values give you a sense of the direction you want to take as a parent. However, keep in mind that reading the compass and seeing the direction in which you want to go is not the same as moving in the direction of your parenting values. Choosing and living a parenting value are two different things. Let's zoom in on this idea in the next section.

Taking Values-Based Parenting Actions

Choosing the parent you want to be is simply the beginning of your new journey as parent; it's the beginning of a 180-degree shift. I was struck, years ago, by something Kelly Wilson (one of the ACT founders) said in a workshop I attended: "Talking about values without actions is like talking about beautiful words taken by the wind." This is a great statement to introduce you to a fundamental ACT skill: values-based behaviors. *Values-based behaviors* in respect to parenting are exactly that: behaviors driven by your parenting values. Throughout this book, the terms values-based behaviors and *values-based actions* will be used interchangeably.

Values-based behaviors are very specific actions you take to live your parenting values; within ACT you are invited to live your values not with your thoughts, memories, sensations, or feelings but with your feet. Specific actions are actions that state exactly what you're going to do, when you're going to do it, how you're going to do it, and where you're going to do it. You can come up with specific values-driven behaviors by remembering to answer the *what, when, how,* and *where* questions.

EXERCISE: Your Parenting Values-Based Behaviors

Pull out your parenting journal, choose a single parenting value you want to work on, and then write down your answers to these questions:

1. What three specific values-based actions am I going to take?

2. When am I going to do them?

3. How often am I going to do them?

4. Where am I going to do them?

Vivian, the mother of a sixteen-year-old daughter struggling with emotional sensitivity, found "being compassionate" extremely important, and she came up with the following responses: "I'm going to schedule one-on-one time with my daughter every weekend, ask her what she would like to do for an hour, and then listen intentionally to her while trying to put myself in her shoes."

Now it's quite likely that even after identifying your parenting values and after stating specific actions you want to take within the relationship with your teen, things may not go well. Most of the parents I work with, like anyone would in their shoes, encounter different types of difficulties when putting their parenting values into action. You're not alone. As it happens to you, it happens to all of us. It's called life.

What Gets in the Way of Living Your Parenting Values?

Vivian noticed that when thinking about spending time with her daughter, Loretta, one-on-one, because of her value of connecting, her mind machine got activated and came up with thoughts like *Loretta is so rejecting of me. She is very selfish and self-absorbed almost all the time. I tried before, and it didn't go well.*

Vivian's situation is a natural one for almost every parent. No matter how hard you try, things don't always go as you hope or wish. And please keep in mind that when things go wrong, it's not about controlling how your teen responds, because you don't have control of it, but it's really about how you handle that rocky moment when things just went south with your vulnerable teen.

When moving toward your values, you may actually find yourself fused with old judgments, rules, past or future thoughts, or stories about yourself or your teen. You may also go through uncomfortable emotions that urge you to use old avoidance strategies, such as the surrenderer, externalizer, pusher, disconnector, or distracter. You may even go to the classic responses of questioning whether those thoughts, memories, urges, and feelings are accurate or not, real or not, or whether you're right and your teen is wrong. Getting hooked on that mind noise, going back to those tricky emotion management strategies, or checking whether what you're thinking or feeling is true or not will quite likely make things worse for you when dealing with your dysregulated teen. So let's do an exercise to figure out those unique blocks you may encounter when taking steps toward your parenting values.

EXERCISE: What's Stopping You?

Grab your parenting journal and see if you can identify the potential internal barriers that may show up for you when taking action toward your parenting values. Here is what Vivian came up with when completing this exercise:

Value: *Being accepting*

Goal: *Asking Loretta about her beliefs on religion at Monday's dinner*

Internal barrier: *Tons of judgment thoughts such as "She's ignorant, doesn't know what she's talking about. She's just a teen being a stubborn teen." Future thoughts: "Nothing will work; she will just shut down as she always does."*

Every time you identify a value and specific goals for it, make sure you also honestly check with yourself about those internal barriers that may get in your way.

Taking a values-based step is an invitation not only to identify the potential obstacles that may show up under your skin but also to pause and choose an ACT response you can rely on when dealing with your teen. Following with our example, Vivian came up with the following

ACT skill: *Naming the judgment machine as "noisy Vivian." Noticing "my time-traveling machine."*

At this point, like Vivian, you're equipped with different ACT skills to handle the internal noise you go through when parenting your vulnerable teen and moving toward your parenting values.

However, putting in action your parenting values to be the best parent possible for your highly sensitive teen requires on extra ingredient: willingness.

Willingness: the Key Ingredient

Willingness is the core ingredient to stop the struggle with those sticky feelings, thoughts, sensations, or memories you go through when dealing with your dysregulated teen; the key is to actually *have them* without acting on them, notice them without pushing them, and name them without denying them. When putting your parenting values in action, willingness is asking yourself the question: *Am I willing to have all types of uncomfortable thoughts, images, memories, feelings, urges, and sensations and still do what matters to me as parent in a given moment with my highly sensitive teen?*

Making this shift may feel counterintuitive in the beginning, because naturally we try to protect ourselves from being in discomfort, and we try to fix our struggle as quickly as possible. The challenge here is that there is no fixing to do when you are having all types of internal experiences when parenting your vulnerable teen, because all the sticky internal noise will come and go, not only once but multiple times, as long as you're moving toward your parenting values. There is only a choice for you to make every time this happens: ask yourself, *Am I willing to have all this internal noise and still choose to do what matters to me as a parent?* The choice is yours.

Summary

In this chapter, you have stepped back from your daily parenting life and identified important qualities you want to cultivate as a parent: your parenting values. You've distinguished them from goals, morals, wishes, and feelings and learned that you live your values with your feet and by taking specific actions. Naturally, when taking steps toward being the parent you want to be, there are going to be all types of internal barriers, such as getting fused with judgmental thoughts, rules, past and future thoughts, and stories or narratives about yourself or your teen, or natural impulses to avoid as much as you can uncomfortable emotions, such as disappointment, powerlessness, and frustration, to name a few. All that internal noise is going to be present, and at the end, it's an invitation to willingly have it and still move toward what matters to you. Change is possible, if you're willing to try.

Weekly Practice: Creating an Action Plan

In your journal, create a parenting-values action plan for the week that includes your values, actions, barriers, willingness, ACT skills to handle your barriers, and outcomes. Under "outcome," you are invited to write down the result of engaging in a parenting values-based action. Doing this exercise on an ongoing basis will help you monitor the direction of your parenting journey so that you can check in with yourself daily whether you're behaving as the parent you want to be.

Keep in mind that keeping track of the behavioral steps you will be taking while working with this book is not about engaging in perfect parenting behaviors but about choosing the type of parent you want to be from moment to moment, especially in moments of conflict with your teen.

You have chosen to read this book because you're raising a teen with emotional vulnerability, and this is not an easy task. If you have read up to this point, you're doing your best to make a difference, but even giving your best doesn't necessarily mean you will get the ideal outcome. Parenting based on your values is not about being a perfect parent but rather about staying committed to striving to be the parent you want to be even when things get rocky. You're going to need more skills than you've learned in this first part. Part 3 is going to teach you the extra skills you need to continue to move toward becoming the parent you want to be. The choice to continue learning new parenting skills is always yours. The choice to become the parent you want to be is always yours too.

PART 3

Making a Shift

CHAPTER 9

"I'm Here, Fully Present": Mindfulness Skills

The beginnings of a chapter can be challenging at times. You sit in front of the computer, you think you're clear about what you need to write, and then the next thing you know, you have spent a couple of hours staring at the computer screen with nothing on it. This is exactly what happened when I started working on this chapter about mindfulness. Ironic, isn't it? When I look back at this moment, I can tell you that my mind had a waterfall of thoughts about my day, my workout routine, lyrics of songs, images of past trips, images of new trips I want to take—the list goes on and on. Even though I intended to write, I wasn't fully present with my writing ideas. Instead, every thought, memory, and image that showed up in my mind pulled me in a different direction. It was as if I were opening different doors in a house and each one of them took me into a different room with different furniture to be appreciated. What was the outcome of my writing time? The screen was 100 percent blank. I was too busy letting my mind take me into a mind trip. I was too busy to be present in the moment. I was too busy to be mindful.

Over the last twenty years, the notion of being mindful or present has become a very popular theme within Western culture in academic settings, pop-psychology publications, and social media. Jon Kabat-Zinn (1990) was the first psychologist to incorporate mindfulness when working with clients with chronic medical conditions. Mindfulness has been applied to the treatment of multiple psychological struggles such as depression, anxiety, chronic pain, and PTSD, and mindfulness can have a positive impact on relationships, such as the relationship with your emotionally dysregulated teen.

What Is Mindfulness?

Because mindfulness is a popular term these days and an important foundational brick within ACT, let's briefly go over some of the most common misconceptions about it:

Myth: the purpose of mindfulness is to reduce stress and anxiety levels. The purpose of mindfulness is to be present and aware of our surroundings and ourselves; when practicing mindfulness, sometimes levels of stress or anxiety are reduced, but that's the plus, the bonus, and not the purpose.

Myth: you can only practice mindfulness if you are in a quiet environment. As Kabat-Zinn (2005) highlighted in his book, *Wherever You Go, There You Are*, mindfulness can be practiced wherever you are, at any time, and in any place. All you need is your intention to be fully present in a given moment. As you will learn in this chapter, practicing mindfulness doesn't involve a quiet place with your eyes closed all the time; that's just one way of practicing being in the present.

Myth: practicing mindfulness is the same as a practicing a religion. Mindfulness has been part of many religious practices: Judaism, Christianity, and Islam, to name a few; however, it's not necessary to be religious to choose to be present in a given moment. People can learn to be mindful in the moment even though they are not affiliated with any religious group. Learning to be present is simply learning to be present.

Myth: mindfulness is all that is needed for helping your struggling teen. While mindfulness or the ability to cultivate your awareness is a pillar within ACT, it's not enough to support your teen struggling with emotion dysregulation and it doesn't replace other necessary skills you have been learning throughout this book and will continue to learn.

Now that we're on the same page about the misconceptions about mindfulness, let's clarify that within ACT, mindfulness is seen as a choice you make to be fully aware or present of what is happening within yourself and your surroundings in a given moment.

Throughout this book, I'll refer to mindfulness skills, *pure awareness* skills, or *present moment* skills interchangeably. For the next section, let's take a look at the relationship between mindfulness and parenting your teen.

From Reactive Parenting to Mindful Parenting

"When you love someone, the best thing you can offer is your presence. How can you love if you are not there?" as Thich Nhat Hanh has said. Relationships, by nature, invite us to be fully there with the person in front of us, and that simple behavior can be both a precious experience and a painful one. Chances are that you have heard this before, as well as the importance of being mindful or fully present with your teen. What's the challenge of doing so when parenting? Much of the time, parents tell me, "Whatever being present means…" and finish their sentence by saying "I just cannot find the time to do it" or "I don't know how to be there when things are so rocky with my teen."

Parenting a highly sensitive teen is a monumental endeavor, full of incredibly sweet, connecting, and caring moments, along with responsibilities, commitments, disappointments, frustration, and even judgment thoughts about yourself and your teen. It's understandable that the busyness of life, plus all of the mind-talk, makes it hard to stay focused in the moment, and you end up being hijacked from that moment.

Practicing mindfulness when parenting is about learning to be *aware* of what's happening inside you by watching your thoughts, feelings, sensations, images, memories, and even impulses when dealing with your teen, without acting on them. By learning pure awareness skills, you will give yourself a chance to step back from a given situation, especially a difficult one, notice your internal experience, and freely choose your parenting response instead of having those intense emotions, judgments, evaluations, rules, or fortune-telling thoughts dictate your behavioral response. You're switching from parenting in automatic pilot mode to parenting in mindful mode. The more you incorporate mindfulness into your parenting life, the more you will learn to be present with your teen, and naturally you will be more skillful at distinguishing what your mind tells you about your teen versus what's really happening with her in a given moment. Distinguishing mind-talk from a present moment experience is a key skill to break the cycle of conflict with your teen, improve your relationship with her, and be the parent you want to be.

Practicing mindfulness can be done informally or traditionally; in this chapter, you will learn both types of practices, so you can have different options to choose from when incorporating mindfulness into your parenting repertoire.

One last word about why mindfulness is important in your parenting life: no relationship can move forward unless we learn to be fully present with the person in front of us; our minds play tricks, and it's a risky trick to get hooked with our mind-talk without checking whether it's helpful to us or not. The relationship with your teen is no exception.

Moving forward, let's start figuring out how to integrate mindfulness in your daily life.

Mindful Parenting in Daily Life

If your life is like the lives of most of the parents I work with, then it's quite likely you spend tons of hours driving your teen, preparing meals, attending sports events, helping with homework, planning family weekends, and doing other countless family activities. The life of a parent is a busy one, and if your teen is struggling with emotional sensitivity, then you need to add hours of therapy, parent coaching, and even practicing skills. It all adds up, and without noticing it, parenting becomes a full-time job without vacation time.

Here is an important observation: as the list of parenting responsibilities grows, the list of opportunities for practicing mindfulness also grows. Practicing mindfulness in your daily life is doable, even if you live in a very busy environment and move at a very fast pace, as many parents do. Here are some exercises for you to start practicing mindfulness while performing daily parenting tasks.

Exercise: Mindfully Driving to Pick Up Your Teen

This is not an ideal setting for practicing, but the fact is that most parents spend a significant amount of hours dropping off and picking up their teens; if this is your case, you have an opportunity to practice mindfulness right away. Before starting this exercise, please read it first and record it in your cell phone or other recording device with a soft voice and at a slow pace; then choose a day and a time to start practicing it. When practicing, it's better if you turn off the radio, so you can be fully engaged. It may seem strange to be in silence at the beginning, as if something is missing, but if possible, allow the silence to be there as a starting point to this exercise. Please avoid practicing this exercise if you see an erratic driver or anything that could potentially be a threat to your safety.

> See if you can start noticing your breathing; notice the sensations in your chest and abdomen with each breath you take in and out. Slowly switch the focus of your attention from your breathing to your body posture. See if you can slowly scan your body from the top to the bottom, starting with your head and moving to your neck, chest, abdomen, arms, hips, legs, and feet. See if you can identify any area of tension, and then relax that particular area. Gently notice any shift in your body as the car moves forward or when you use the brake and the car pauses. Notice the intersection points in your body that connect different body areas. Notice your feet against the floor mat. If your mind starts wandering and coming up with thoughts about this exercise or images or any other type of thoughts, kindly name those thoughts for what they are, *thoughts*, and bring your awareness back to the act of driving.
>
> With both hands on the steering wheel, notice the sensation of your skin touching the wheel. Is it soft or hard? Is it rough or smooth? Is it hot or cold? You can even slowly move both of your hands, up and down, while touching the wheel and noticing these sensations.
>
> See if you can notice other movements of driving, such as how it feels when pushing the brake or the accelerator again. If your mind drifts to your to-do list or any other distracting thought or image, gently bring your awareness back to the act of driving.

Now slowly switch the focus of your attention from the act of driving to the surroundings outside the car. Can you describe the colors of the cars you see around you? Do they have stickers? What are the car models? If you're driving on the freeway, you can start counting the number of billboards you pass while driving, noticing the speed of the traffic, or noticing the space between you and the car in front of you. If you're driving on city streets, see if you can pay attention to the street names, the types of properties you see, the numbers of the houses, or the moments you pause because of a red light. See if you can notice the sounds of the passing tires on the pavement or the subtle movement of the car driving on different pavements, the fragments of music coming from other cars, or even the sound of your own or another car's engine.

After a couple of moments of practicing this mindful exercise, kindly let it go, and simply take a mental note of any reaction you had to it.

How was it for you to be fully present when driving? How was it for you to be fully present for one thing at a time?

Here's another mindful exercise that can be practiced every time you're making a meal, and you can start practicing it at any point of preparing the meal.

Exercise: Mindfully Preparing a Meal

For this exercise, read the instructions first for a sense of the direction, and then practice it.

1. Stand with your feet about hip-width apart and then push them against the floor to start.

2. Gently and slowly roll your shoulders back and forth multiple times and notice that particular movement in your body.

3. Notice the quality of your breathing every time you inhale and exhale, and see if you can even notice the subtleties of your breathing, like the temperature or the pace of it.

4. Gently shift your attention from your breathing to the specific cooking activity you are doing in the moment, even if it's simply grabbing the ingredients from the refrigerator or choosing cooking utensils.

5. Pay attention to all the ingredients in front of you by carefully studying each one of them. For a couple of moments, describe slowly to yourself their colors, shapes, smell, and textures, and see if you can even discover characteristics that you didn't see before. Is that ingredient smooth or rough? How does this one's shape feel in your hand? Can you feel the weight of the ingredient in your hands? Do you distinguish its individual smell?

6. Notice the sounds that show up every time you're manipulating these cooking ingredients.

7. See if you can go back to the beginning of this exercise and repeat these directions as a curious activity, inviting yourself to be fully present with it.

When you're done, slowly take a breath, and notice any reaction to this mindful activity.

You can practice being mindful during other daily parenting tasks, such as doing the laundry, doing the dishes, shopping for clothing with your teen, or even when going to the doctor for a medical appointment. All you need is your commitment to be present in the moment and fully notice any activity you're engaged in.

Let's switch gears now to some more traditional mindfulness exercises.

EXERCISE: Mindfulness of Sensations, Emotions, Images, and Thoughts

For this exercise, it's better if you read the directions slowly, record them in your cell phone or other recording device, and then start practicing. Find yourself a comfortable position in a quiet environment, so you can fully focus on this exercise for the next ten minutes.

Sit in a relaxed position, or if better for you, lean your body against a wall, and start noticing the passing sensations of the air as you breathe in and breathe out. Gently bring your awareness to your chest and abdomen as they rise and fall while you inhale and exhale. Notice the pace of your breathing while you focus on the sensation of air as it enters your nostrils, moves through your body, and leaves it a few moments later.

Because your mind is prone to wonder about many different things, it's natural that you may find yourself distracted by various thoughts or images in this moment; do your best to notice these thoughts as they come, and even if they're images, gently name each one of them by silently saying to yourself *thought* every time you notice them; then, without responding to them or getting hooked on them, let them drift by, like clouds in the sky, and gently shift your attention back to your breathing as the anchor of this exercise.

In the next couple of moments, shift the focus of your attention from your breathing to your feelings. See if you can notice how you are feeling in this precise moment and, with a pinch of curiosity, notice whether the feeling is pleasant or unpleasant, comfortable or uncomfortable. Can you name your emotion for what it is? If so, say silently to yourself the name of the emotion, and if you find yourself struggling to name the emotion, gently move along with this exercise and see if you can notice the sensation that comes with this emotion in your body. Can you localize this sensation in your body? Can you notice what particular body area holds this sensation? Is it in your upper body or lower body? Can you describe this sensation silently to yourself, without looking at it as good or bad but simply describing the quality of it using words such as *tingling*, *itching*, or other qualifiers for it?

And if another emotion or sensation arises, describe it as you did with the previous one and observe how your emotional landscape changes while this exercise progresses, from moment to moment. Keep noticing the sensations and emotions rising and ebbing for a couple of moments; continue to name thoughts as *thoughts* as they come and go. Finally, bring your attention one more time back to your breathing, noticing the quality of each breath as it goes in and out, noticing the quality of every time you inhale and exhale, and then slowly let this exercise go, and bring yourself back into this moment.

Afterward, pick up your parenting journal, and take a moment to reflect on your reactions to this exercise.

EXERCISE: Mindfulness of the Emotional Rollercoaster

This exercise is based on Blaise Aguirre and Gillian Galen's exercise (2013), and it takes approximately fifteen minutes from the beginning to the end. You are invited to record it with a soft and slow tone of voice, and then listen to it and take the steps indicated. You will also need your parenting journal to complete it, since the exercise goes back and forth between noticing an internal experience and writing down your reactions to it.

Allow yourself to rest your eyes by closing them, and gently direct your awareness to your breathing. Allow yourself to notice every time you breathe in and out, and see if you can give yourself a chance to be present in this moment, as best you can, while focusing on your breathing.

For the next couple of moments, recall a sad memory you went through with your teen; it can be a sad situation that happened recently, a couple of weeks ago, or even months ago. Do your best to choose one of those memories without getting stuck on whether it's the right memory or not, but bringing the image of this sad moment into your mind as vividly as possible. Do your best to recall it and even relive it as if it were happening right now in this precise moment, so you can clearly see it in your mind. Hold on to this image for a bit and see if you notice the thoughts you had about your teen while experiencing the sadness of the moment. How did you think about your teen in that moment? What thoughts came to you about your teen in that sad moment? Notice any restrictions in your body, and other emotional responses. After noticing your experience, let this image fade from your mind, open your eyes, turn off the tape, and write down in your parenting journal the thoughts that came up about your teen in that sad memory.

Turn on the tape and close your eyes again and kindly focus your awareness into your breathing, and notice the passing sensations of the air as you inhale and exhale. Allow yourself to be grounded by your breathing before moving forward with this exercise.

Kindly see if you can recall a moment in which you got angry at your teen. Don't worry if it's something that happened recently or a long time ago, but simply do your best to recall one of those moments you want to work on for this mindful exercise. And as you did with the first memory, see if you can imagine that angry memory as vividly as possible, noticing the unique character-istics of it the best you can, and while holding on to this angry image, notice the thoughts you were having about your teen in that moment. Did you have any criticizing or judgmental thoughts? Did you have a narrative about your teen as a person? How did your body respond in that moment of anger? See if you can notice any sensations in your body as this experience progresses. Try to let it go, slowly open your eyes, turn off the tape, and write down the thoughts that came up about your teen in your parenting journal, one by one.

Turn on the tape and close your eyes one last time. Press your feet against the floor as though your feet are the trunk of a tree, and slowly shift your attention to your breathing one more time, allow-ing yourself to be present in this moment.

Stay with your breathing for a couple of moments, and then see if for this last part of the exercise you can recall a moment of con-nection you had with your teen. And as you did with the other memories, do your best to bring this moment of connection into your mind as vividly as possible, paying attention to the uniqueness of it and holding on to it for a couple of moments. Gently, and while still focusing on this image, see if you can notice the different thoughts you had about your teen while experiencing this moment of connection. How did you think about your teen? What thoughts came to your mind while holding on to this memory of connection with your teen? Take a final look at your thoughts, then take a deep and slow breath, let go of this image, open your eyes, turn off the tape, and write down the thoughts that came up in this last part of this exercise.

Spend some time reviewing the different thoughts you have written about your teen while you were moving through different memories of sadness, anger, and connection with your teen during this exercise. Did you notice any differences between the thoughts that show up about your teen? Did you think of your teen differently because of the different emotions you went through?

Emotions will naturally color your thoughts about your teen, and without realizing it you may stop seeing your teen for who she is but for what the emotion tells you she is. Mindfully noticing your emotions allows you to step back and learn to have the emotion for what it is without letting it dictate who your teen is.

Mindfully Communicating with Your Teen

Up to this point, you have learned the *why* of mindfulness and how to practice it during typical daily activities and in traditional exercises that help you to be aware of your thoughts, sensations, feelings, memories, and urges for what they are, without getting hooked on them. Here is a different setting in which mindfulness can be practiced: while having a conversation with your teen. Although listening and talking seem like pretty easy skills, they both require intention and commitment to stay present and hear what your teen is communicating in the moment.

Are you ready to show up for and hear your teen 100 percent? If so, keep moving forward with these suggestions for practicing mindful communication her; you can practice the suggested recommendations anytime you're talking to her, even if it's for a short period of time. Before beginning to integrate mindful communication, put aside your go-to physical distractions (cell phone, computer, talk shows, podcasts, TV remote), so they don't kidnap you. If you're not ready to practice mindful communicating, before making a decision whether to continue or not with this exercise, check in with yourself to see what thoughts, images, or sensations are showing up for you—for example, *It's not going to work* or *Nothing is going to change* or *This is clichéd*. Can you distinguish whether those thoughts, images, or sensations are old or new? Can you notice what those stories are pushing you to do? Is your mind asking you to stay or to avoid? To move forward or backward? And finally, can you check in with yourself about what you really want to do in this moment? The decision is yours. It's understandable if you're not ready to practice this mindful communicating exercise, as long as you're making an intentional choice and not an automatic one.

EXERCISE: Communicating Mindfully

When talking to your teen, start by noticing your teen's facial expression. Are your teen's eyebrows up or down? How does your teen's forehead look? Can you notice the pace of her speech? Is it fast or slow? Can you notice the rhythm of the speech? Can you notice the pitch of her voice? While listening, check any impulse to interject or share your thoughts before your teen finishes her sentences. Do you have an urge to share your own take on things or your own story? Do you feel the urge to offer advice to your teen?

Take a breath before responding. Check again with yourself about whether you are willing to continue practicing mindful communication with your teen. If you are, then ask clarifying questions, show curiosity, and present your point of view, not from a place of trying to convince your teen of something but rather from a place of sharing.

Mindfully communicating with your teen can be difficult. Your mind will wander and throw all types of thoughts and urges at you; these will likely be distracting. At times, your mind will succeed and take you into automatic pilot mode. Keep in mind that the more you practice being present with your teen, the better you're going to be at noticing your thought machine and strong urges and bringing yourself back to the conversation with your teen in that moment.

Summary and Looking Ahead

Mindfulness, or pure awareness, is a skill and a choice you make to be present with yourself and your surroundings in a given moment, even when uncomfortable memories, thoughts, images, urges, sensations, and feelings show up. Mindfulness is a core skill that will help you to shift from reactive to effective parenting. You can practice mindfulness in your daily life through different activities, including running errands, or in quiet environments by finding a comfortable position and following guided mindfulness exercises.

As an ongoing mindfulness practice, identify the three most common activities you do during the week, such as grocery shopping or washing dishes, and voila! You are ready to start practicing mindfulness. As Jon Kabat-Zinn said, you can practice mindfulness wherever you are, wherever you go.

CHAPTER 10

"I See You":
Appreciation Skills

Let's start this chapter by acknowledging the nature of all relationships and what makes them successful. Relationships are living entities that evolve, morph, and transform, and to be successful, they require attention. No relationship will survive without adjustments, changes, and caring behaviors from the people involved in it. The relationship with your teen requires attention, and because your teen is struggling with emotion dysregulation problems, it needs extra attention. By paying extra attention to how the relationship with your teen is going, making changes when possible and needed, and accepting that you don't have control over your teen's behaviors, you will be improving your relationship and teaching your teen how to maintain healthy relationships.

Here is a skill for creating a healthy relationship with your teen: appreciation. The term *appreciation* comes from two Latin words: *ad*, which means "toward," and *pretium*, which means "worth, value, price." Based on those roots, appreciation essentially means to see the value in other people's experiences, behaviors, objects, and even situations. In the relationship with your teen, appreciating him means learning to see him as a whole person and not only as a person who makes mistakes, shows problematic behaviors, or is full of faults.

Appreciating Your Teen

Within ACT, appreciation is another behavior that can be practiced, rehearsed, and developed at all times. However, some parents

I have worked with get fused with the thoughts *If I praise my teen too much, I'll spoil him; he will learn to do things just because of the reward or recognition from others; he shouldn't be appreciated for something he is supposed to do.* Let's take a moment to see the effect of that thought on the relationship with your teen.

EXERCISE: Appreciation Bumps

Let's take a look at those appreciation bumps in your parenting behavior.

1. Grab your parenting journal and recall a time when your teen did or said something that made you smile, such as getting a good grade or turning down a friend's invitation to smoke weed. Do your best to describe that particular situation in your journal.

2. Then write down what you do when holding on to the belief that *If I praise my teen too much, I'll spoil him. He will learn to do things just because of the reward or recognition from others.*

3. Next, write down the short-term and long-term consequences to the relationship with your teen of behaving based on that belief.

4. Then answer the question, do those behaviors take you toward the parent you want to be?

After reading your responses, check for yourself the workability of your parenting responses when getting fused with the rule "I shouldn't praise my teen."

If you're still fused with this antipraising thought, there are two things I would like to share with you. First of all, praising is simply a form of appreciating the ideal behaviors you observe in another, and it creates a healthy communication loop between you and your teen when you give positive feedback for appropriate behaviors. Well-adjusted teens come from homes where parents provide an emotional environment that has both positive feedback and limit setting (Patterson and Forgatch 2005). Secondly, because of emotion dysregulation problems, your teen perceives negative comments more intensely than others, and without receiving any appreciation, praise, or positive feedback, he is deprived of learning how to modify and adjust his behavior in regard to others, as we all naturally do in relationships.

Without receiving positive feedback, your teen still needs to make sense of others' behaviors and therefore can quickly get fused with his mind-talk on stories, evaluations, or fortune-telling thoughts about what works and what doesn't for the other person. Getting fused with his mind-talk and behaving without really learning what the other person needs, wants, or desires is learning to behave like a robot. Learning to interact with others requires learning to receive positive and negative feedback in order to organize our social behavior, and this is a core interpersonal skill, especially when there are emotional-sensitivity issues and the emotional switch goes on and off at any time.

Every time your teen behaves in a way that is helpful and appropriate and he does not receive direct feedback from you, he misses the opportunity to develop a natural sense of how to behave with you or with others. Without being appreciated, your teen is exposed to an intense sense of loneliness, isolation, and even abandonment, because he won't learn to organize his interpersonal responses when dealing with others.

While reading this book, I'm going to ask you to make changes in your parenting behaviors, but no one can make those changes for you. Here is a moment of choice for you: will you continue getting fused with those anti-appreciating thoughts, or will you learn a new parenting behavior that could improve the relationship with your teen? The choice is yours.

Here is the first step to appreciate your teen: catching him doing good.

Catching Your Teen Doing Good

John Gottman and Nan Silver (1999) are two therapists and researchers who conducted the longest study in the history of couples therapy in the United States. Their clinical and research work has significantly influenced the way therapists work with couples these days, and ultimately, their findings have been critical in helping hundred and hundreds of couples to survive the challenges of loving each other. Among many of their findings about what sustains healthy relationships, here is an important one: successful relationships have a five-to-one ratio of positive interactions to negative ones. This basically means that every negative interaction needs to be balanced with five positive ones; positive interactions can take the form of physical touch, smiles, spontaneous kisses, compliments, and any other sign of positive regard.

Gottman and Silver's work indicates that stable relationships have some level of negativity, but it's the positive interactions that nourish the relationship, like making deposits in an emotional bank account. Positive and negative interactions are necessary in any relationship, are the foundation for handling differences and disagreements, and ultimately are key for fostering a healthy relationship. The relationship with your teen is not exempt from the benefits of balancing positive and negative interactions, and there is no one better than you for teaching this skill to your teen.

Now that you have learned the *what* and *why* of appreciation skills, let me introduce you to the *how* of appreciation skills.

Let's NAP: Notice, Appreciate, and Praise Verbally

Here are three specific steps: notice, appreciate, and praise verbally immediately. You can remember these steps by using the simple acronym NAP.

Noticing is simply about describing a specific behavior, such as your teen picking up his clothes from the floor.

Appreciating is recognizing the value of your teen's behavior.

Praising is letting him know as soon as possible that you see the value in his behavior. The more specific the praise is, the more you're creating opportunities for your teen to engage in effective behaviors. Praising statements can start with "I like that you...," "I enjoy it when you...," "I appreciate that you...," or "It makes me smile that you..."

As an example, after Aidan made an explicit choice to appreciate his teen, he made an extra effort to catch him doing good and came up with the following appreciation statement: "Sammy, it's great to see that you picked up your clothes from the floor today. Kudos to you."

Here are some other examples of specific praising statements:

- "It makes me smile that you did the dishes without my asking."

- "I enjoyed it when you included your cousin in every game you played last night after dinner."

- "I appreciated that your science homework was really carefully printed this morning."

For the next couple of days, do your best to practice your NAP skills every time you see your teen doing something you want to see happening more often even though it's a small behavior, such as him saying "thank you" or opening the door of the car for you or putting the cell phone face down on the table when sitting down for dinner or just asking nicely for a snack. You will be surprised by the effect that explicit appreciation can have on the relationship with your teen. Can you shoot for the five-to-one ratio of positive to negative interactions in the relationship with your teen?

Watch Out for Fake Statements!

Charles Schwab was very well known within his company for bringing out enthusiasm in his employees; when he was asked about his secret, he said, "sincere appreciation." Here is something we can infer from Schwab's statement that applies to the relationship with your teen: cheesy, false, over-the-top, or appreciating statements that are too general are not helpful. For example, telling your teen "You did a spectacular job" is not helpful at all. Using words such as "spectacular" without mentioning a specific behavior won't help your teen feel appreciated or encourage him to engage in a desirable behavior. It is ultra important to use statements that really communicate to your teen exactly what you're appreciating in his behavior.

Here is another principle to consider when using appreciation skills: telling your teen a couple of hours later that he did a great job when picking up his sister from school or when organizing the recycling bins in the garage is not as effective as telling him in the moment when you catch him doing good. Of course, if you're not there to observe this behavior in the moment, praising the behavior as soon as possible is still helpful.

Appreciating Your Teen's Struggles

Most of us have been taught to focus only on positive things, and our culture constantly reinforces this tendency, perpetuating the idea that life is mostly full of happy, good, and positive moments. Let's pause for a moment and reflect on this message: up to this point, has your parenting life been full of only positive moments? Quite likely your parenting life has both sweet, loving, joyful moments and painful, challenging, and difficult ones.

Within ACT, you're invited to practice appreciation skills at all times, not only when your teen is engaging in appropriate behaviors but also when he's struggling with emotional responses, such as frustration, sadness, or jealousy because of his homework, a character in a movie, or even the lyrics of a song, to name a few triggering situations. Being present with painful experiences is not about dwelling or rethinking on them in a masochistic manner but simply about recognizing that the struggle is real and it's there.

It's important that you learn to notice and teach your teen how all emotions, including uncomfortable and painful ones, will come and go as clouds in the sky; we can learn to watch them and have them without becoming them.

You may be asking yourself, how can I appreciate my teen's moment of struggle or painful feelings? Here is your response: you do it by noticing and describing your teen's emotional experience for what it is. For instance, when your teen gets sad about the puppy not wanting to sleep with him and that makes him feel rejected, notice and describe that moment by using words like "Tommy, I see that you grabbed the puppy, so he could stay with you during the night, but he just left, and I see your face—that's a bummer." You don't have to agree, like, or feel positive about your teen's reactions; just noticing and describing them to him are specific ways to turn up your appreciation skills and let him know that you see the difficulty he's going through in that particular situation.

Here is a special consideration when dealing with not-so-pleasant emotions: if an uncomfortable emotion is repetitive, more consistent than others, and shows up for you more often than not, then see if you can make room for that emotion by noticing how it feels in your body, discovering whether it is static or not, giving it a name, and asking yourself *What is this emotion trying to communicate to me?* Learning to appreciate painful emotions is also recognizing their value in our emotional life. These repetitive uncomfortable emotions are like units of information and may have a different purpose in your life, such as reminding you of what's important, bringing your attention to changes or decisions you need to make.

Appreciation skills build on the mindfulness skills you learned in chapter 9; mindfulness, at its core, asks you to stay intentionally present with your experience, whatever the experience is, and that includes all types of comfortable and not-so-pleasant reactions.

Summary and Looking Ahead

Appreciation skills help you to see the value of your teen's emotional experiences; using appreciation skills during times of struggle means you get the sweet and the sour, the good and the bad, the beauty and the ugliness, without running away or pushing any of it away.

Letting your teen know that you appreciate every appropriate behavior will help him to develop a very important interpersonal skill: receiving and giving feedback. You can continue practicing your appreciation skills with your teen by using the acronym NAP: notice, appreciate, and praise verbally immediately; keep in mind that praising is effective when it's specific and genuine.

And finally, appreciating skills are also about noticing and seeing value in moments of struggle that you, your teen, and every human being go through in life. Sometimes those repetitive painful emotions are indicators of changes we need to make.

Appreciation skills are the foundation for cultivating empathic behaviors with your teen, and that's the next skill for you to learn.

CHAPTER 11

"I Get It, It's Hard": Empathy Skills

Did you know that we are biologically wired to identify emotionally with another person's feelings? Our brain has a particular type of neurons, called *mirror neurons*, that explain our empathic responses to another's pain: when a person in front of us is showing anger, frustration, or joy, our mirror neurons light up in our brains like a Christmas tree. Isn't that fascinating? If we are wired to put ourselves in the shoes of another person, what happens between you and your teen in the middle of those countless arguments in which you don't hear each other and don't see the other's point of view?

When working with parents of teens struggling with emotional reactivity, it's as if I were working with emotional firefighters. They're doing their best to calm fire after fire with their teens, while going through a full chain of emotions themselves, including frustration, hopelessness, confusion, and disconnection. This is a very exhausting job for any parent, and unfortunately, it's like a full-time job for some of you.

I can sincerely tell you that your parenting job is not an easy one, and it's understandable that because you are in constant crisis mode, you may naturally go on automatic pilot for handling conflicts with your teen or any interaction you have with her. The challenge is that unless you make a shift from automatic pilot mode to a strategic mode of handling your teen's behaviors, you are perpetuating a cycle of disconnection between the two of you in which neither of you sees the struggle of the other. It's as if you both were unempathic with each other; you both only see conflict in the relationship.

I'm sure you have heard the word "empathy" before, and it's quite likely you would agree about the importance of having empathy in all relationships, not only in the one with your teen. *Empathy* is not just a nice word but also a behavior that can be learned and practiced, as any other skill. Empathy is the skill that will allow you and your teen to notice each other's emotional struggle, and from that place of recognition and acceptance, you can choose your values-based behaviors.

Three Components of Empathy

Scientist Daniel Goleman (1995) sees empathy as an important quality of emotional intelligence. Empathy involves three components: you understand the other's struggle on a thought level, you put yourself emotionally in the other person's shoes, and you take action to alleviate that struggle. It's like telling your teen "I understand how you think, how you feel, and I want to do something about it." Now, if this is what empathy is about from a scientific point of view, then what are the misconceptions people have about it?

Three Myths About Empathy

Let's briefly go over some of the misconceptions about empathy as they apply to parenting skills:

Myth 1: Either you're empathic or you're not empathic as a parent. The work of different neuroscientists, such as Goleman (1995), Daniel Siegel (1999), and others, has fundamentally confirmed that we're neurologically wired to connect. Every time we interact, our brains naturally go into action mode, which shows up in our social and interpersonal behavior with others. Because of this neurological predisposition, empathy is a skill that can be developed if you're willing to learn how to do it. It's not whether you're empathic or not as a parent; you can learn empathic behaviors like any other skill.

Myth 2: Empathy is all about showing all your emotions to your teen. Showing emotional attunement to your teen's emotional rollercoaster doesn't mean that you have to show high levels of emotional reactivity too. Practicing empathic behaviors involves self-regulation of your own emotions so you can be fully present with your teen and actually show her that even when having an intense emotional experience, you can choose how to behave.

Myth 3: Empathy is a female attribute. Although there is a very popular social perception that women are more empathic than men, recent neuropsychological studies have indicated that the differences in empathic behaviors between men and women are unrelated to any neurological predisposition. This basically means that science shows us that both men and women are wired to experience empathy, but through socialization, family upbringing, and schooling, these behaviors are more reinforced in women than in men.

Now that we have covered what empathy is and the most common myths about empathy applied to parenting, and you know that you're already wired to empathically connect with your teen, why don't you learn the basics of empathic behaviors?

Foundational Bricks of Empathy: Presence and Curiosity

You cannot be empathic without a pinch of curiosity, and you cannot be curious without being fully present with your teen. Being present with your teen is being fully there with her by mindfully paying attention to how she's talking to you and what she's talking about. Being present with your teen sounds easy, but given the myriad of thoughts, images, to-do lists, errands to run, and feelings that you go through on a daily basis, it can become quite challenging; it requires *radical willingness* to do it, 100 percent, all the way. It's as if you were turning the attention switch on when being with your teen. When you're present with her, then you can be curious about her.

Curious behaviors are the ones that start with the thought *What am I missing when talking to my teen?* Curious behaviors are important at all times, but they are particularly important when your teen is sharing something distressing with you. Curious behaviors translate into approaching the conversation with your teen as if you were actually Googling something about her that you want to know more about in that moment. You ask more and more questions until you get it, even if you disagree with her take on things.

For instance, Dennis frequently asks Bradley about the bands she likes to listen to, what new songs they have, and he even asks about the specific lyrics of the songs. Here is the tricky part: Bradley loves those "downer songs" that describe the darkest possible feelings a person can experience: songs about death, grief, and loss. Naturally, when Dennis starts this conversation, he has a pit in his stomach, a feeling of dread, and quickly his mind brings up the thought *That's awful. Bradley needs to hear something more uplifting, not that depressive crap.* He also notices some fears about what else he will have to hear Bradley say, and he notices again the thoughts *Oh boy, among all the things I have to do, the last thing I have time for is to hear those crappy lyrics.* However, Dennis makes an extra effort to mindfully notice those thoughts, name them as coming from "the dark side" (because of his love for the Star Wars movies), and with intention and curiosity, he asks Bradley another question about those songs. Dennis's parenting value is to learn about his son the best he can, especially while he's a teenager. He mindfully recognizes and labels his own mind-talk, the emotions that come along when living his parenting value, and then chooses to ask Bradley another question.

EXERCISE: Practicing Curiosity with Your Teen

Here is an exercise for you to practice curious behaviors: get together with your teen and ask intentionally about a particular interest she has. During the conversation with your teen, watch out for the "I know it all" thoughts or negative judgment thoughts that your mind may be coming up with; you can defuse from those anti-empathic thoughts by acknowledging them first, naming them, **Here come my anti-empathic thoughts**, and finally choosing a parenting response that will help you to have the relationship you want to have with your teen. After you complete this exercise, write down in your parenting journal any reaction you notice.

Being mindfully present and curious with your teen are the key prerequisites for learning empathic behaviors. If you step back, look again at the interactions with your teen, and keep in mind that parental empathy is about putting yourself in your teen's shoes, then you may have more room to make a choice about how to handle sticky situations with her.

Teens who suffer with emotional sensitivity often want their struggle to be seen instead of negatively judged, appreciated instead of minimized, and discovered rather than quickly solved. This is not easy for any parent in the midst of an argument, but it is not impossible either.

The Four As to Practice Empathy with Your Teen

Here are some specific principles to help you practice empathic behaviors with your teen: ask, accept, appreciate verbally your teen's struggle, and ask directly what you can do to help your teen in that moment. You can easily remember these behaviors by memorizing them as the four As.

Ask curious questions about the difficulties your teen is going through. Ask questions about her thoughts, emotions, fears, or wishes about the situation. Curious questions are usually open-ended questions that require a response instead of monosyllabic answers such as "yes" or "no"; open-ended questions include "why," "where," "what," "who," or "how." Ask questions along the lines of "What makes it so hard right now?" "What would make it worse?" "How would it be if you could make it the way you want it to be?" "Can you tell me more about X?"

Accept your teen's reality. Accept that whatever your teen is sharing as upsetting is very real for her: it's her reality in that precise moment. You don't have to agree with how your teen feels or thinks, or what she wants to do, in order to show empathy.

Appreciate by verbally acknowledging and paraphrasing your teen's struggle. This includes whatever is interesting or causing pain to your teen—for example, statements such as "It's really cool you like the lyrics of that song, because they really talk about tough feelings" or "It really sucks that Stefanie texted you back using only two emojis and not five. That's quite upsetting. I get it why you may feel like she doesn't like you."

Ask directly what you can do to help your teen in that moment. Ask how you can help her with her particular struggle. You can ask questions such as, "What can I do to help right now?"

If you put in practice the four As, you will become very skillful at putting yourself in your teen's shoes. Showing your teen empathy when she's struggling, with whatever she's struggling with, will improve your relationship with her, because you get her and are showing her how to create healthy relationships.

EXERCISE: Practicing Empathic Statements

Pick up your parenting journal and come up with empathic statements for these situations:

1. Your teen screams at you because you have just said, "No. It is not okay to go to a party that is unsupervised." Your teen says, "I hate you! My friends will make fun of me over this."

2. Your teen says, "Mom, it doesn't make sense that just because I didn't pass my driver's test twice, because of small things, I'm being forced to get a job just because you say so."

3. You teen says, "When you asked me how I'm doing, it's a double-edged sword, since I know you will start preaching to me about dropping out of the university and about how much time I spend with my boyfriend. You don't understand that my boyfriend keeps me alive."

4. Your teen says, "Tony just broke up with me. I feel like killing myself right now. I don't know how I'm going to go through high school without him. I should just drop everything."

The more you practice empathic statements, the more skillful you're going to be to deal with your teen.

It's time to learn a more complex empathy skill that requires you to be fully present and open with your teen, so you can directly learn from her and not from what your mind tells you she's going through.

Practice Empathic Learning

Here is the rationale for practicing empathic learning: your teen struggles as much as you do, and unless you learn directly from her about her pain, there is no way you can teach her how to handle difficult moments in a skillful manner and in preparation for what life will require from her.

EXERCISE: Practicing Empathic Learning

Here is an exercise to practice empathic learning with your teen. It has three different parts: in the first part, you will learn about your teen; in the second part, your teen will learn about you; and the third part is for you to practice putting yourself in your teen's shoes.

First part: in a moment in which both of you are relatively getting along, ask your teen the following questions about your relationship with her.

1. "What's one of the difficulties you struggle with in our relationship?"

2. "What do you see, hear, or remember about it?"

3. "How does it make you feel when you and I struggle with X?"

4. "What do you think could happen if things continue being rocky between us?"

5. "Is there something you need from me to handle X?"

6. "Is there a specific action you think could be helpful to get unstuck in dealing with X?"

When asking your teen the above questions, make sure to practice the four As: ask, accept, appreciate her struggle, and ask how you can help when she responds! Let your teen know that you will take some time to think about this and get back to her.

Second part: let your teen know about your emotional inner life in regard to your relationship with her by completing the following sentences as a starting point:

"My biggest struggle in our relationship is..." (describe the struggle behaviorally and avoid globalizations about your teen as a character: "lazy," "slob," and so on).

"I feel..."

"I'm concerned this..."

"I would like..."

Third part: privately grab your parenting journal and complete the following sentences with regard to the situation you just discussed with your teen:

"If I were in my teen's shoes, I would feel..."

"If I were in my teen's shoes, I would think..."

"If I were in my teen's shoes, I would have the urges to..."

Make sure you come up with a tentative solution to your teen's struggle regarding her needs, fears, and specific requests in the first part of the exercise, even if it's a temporary one. Learning from your teen directly and sharing with her what you go through in regard to your relationship makes you a real person instead of an authority figure who only prescribes behaviors. No one is better than you to teach your teen how be empathic with others.

When practicing empathic learning, watch out for the judgment machine or past- and future- oriented thoughts getting activated; if you see them showing up, do your best to turn up your defusion dial: notice them, name them, and bring yourself back to your teen and this exercise. Notice that the exercise above focuses on one difficulty that you share, since you don't want to start a battle of words with your teen by discussing a laundry list of challenges or complex situations. The purpose of this exercise on empathic learning is for both of you to learn from each other's struggles, because in moments of conflict, it's quite likely that you don't see each other's difficulties.

Empathy Skills Blocks

Being present, curious, and showing empathic behaviors to your teen will certainly improve your relationship with her; it will naturally take a couple of trials for you to get in the habit of doing it. Learning or improving any behavioral skill also requires being prepared for potential blocks in the road, and that's what this section is about. Over the years, I have witnessed three common empathy blocks for parents: problem-solving behaviors, denying the teen's feelings, and lecturing or advising their teen. Let's go over each of these empathy blocks.

Problem-solving behaviors include cheerful and solution-oriented statements such as "Everything is going to be okay," "Let's just watch a movie, so you don't have to think about it," or "Don't worry about not being invited to the camping trip. I'm sure there will be other camping trips for you."

Parents may also deny their teen's feelings about their experience by using correcting or minimizing statements, such as "Actually, this is not what happened, if you recall…" or "I don't understand why this is so upsetting to you. It's actually not a big deal." The more you deny your teen's emotions, the more your teen is noticing and experiencing them.

Finally, lecturing or advising with comments such as "I don't want to say this, but I told you so," "If you had listened to me, this wouldn't be happening," or "If you were nicer to those kids, you wouldn't have to deal with this" will make it harder for any teen to respond positively; in difficult moments, your teen, like anyone else, is simply not in the best place to learn anything.

Here is your challenge: can you notice those urges to try to solve the problem, deny it, or teach your teen about her troubles? If you notice yourself having any of those urges, ground yourself with your breathing, pause, and see if you can instead show an empathic behavior. Urges, like other sensations or emotions, are temporary, and they can't take over the moment unless we feed them. If you notice those impulses, you can even shift your facial expression into a curious one by lifting your eyebrows and opening your eyes when talking to your teen. You can also practice defusion skills from those problem-solving and lecturing thoughts by naming them first, imagining you're placing them on the cars of a commercial train, and seeing the train moving on the train track until it's gone from your sight.

Remember, the more you practice empathic behaviors, the more you're modeling for your teen how to connect with others and create long-lasting relationships.

Summary and Looking Ahead

Being present and curious with your teen are prerequisites for empathy skills. Empathy skills require that you understand how your teen thinks about a difficult situation, get a feeling for her struggle, and then attempting to do something about it as if you were the one going through the experience. To practice empathy skills, remember to use the four As: ask, accept, acknowledge your teen's experience verbally, and ask directly what you can do to help your teen in that moment.

Watch out for potential blocks for delivering empathy skills, such as fusion with myths about empathy and urges to solve the problem, deny it, or teach your teen about her feelings. Within ACT, as you are learning throughout this book, a key question is to look at the impact of your thoughts, sensations, images, urges, feelings, and actions and whether or not they help you to move toward creating the relationship you want to have with your teen. So if you find yourself buying into any of those myths as if you were fused with them, ask yourself this key question: what happens to the relationship with your teen when you rigidly hold on to that myth and behave based on that?

To practice empathic behaviors on an ongoing basis, identify a situation in which you struggled with your teen and write it down in your journal at the top of the page; then draw a line dividing the page into two columns. On the left side, write how you felt, thought, any urges you had, and what you did; on the right side, write how your teen may have felt, thought, what urges your teen may have had, and what your teen did.

Keep in mind that you can approach your teen's likes, dreams, and struggles by getting fused with the thought *I know exactly what she's going through*, or you can ask, *What am I missing this time?* Your choice.

CHAPTER 12

"Let's Talk": Assertiveness Skills

"I would like you to be more affectionate," says Catherine to her husband Mark, while they're walking in the streets of the San Francisco Bay Area. As soon as she finishes saying those words, Mike notices the thoughts *Does she want me to send her flowers? Would she like me to get her the purse she showed me the other day? Or does she want more movie nights?* As the walk progresses, Mark does his best to continue to be engaged in the conversation, but at the end of their walk he realizes that he didn't understand what Catherine meant by asking him to be more affectionate. So he decides to ask his wife what she meant by that comment, and the next thing he hears is "Sweetie, you will figure out. We have been together for over ten years…" Mark can't stop noticing all the new questions showing up in his mind trying to make sense of Catherine's response.

Whether it's a romantic relationship, a friendship, a sibling, or parent-teen relationship, assertiveness skills are necessary for everyone and in every relationship. We constantly communicate with each other for different purposes, and unless we develop a style of communication that facilitates clarity in the conversation, it can be very frustrating and unsatisfying for everyone involved.

By incorporating assertiveness skills in your parenting job, you're modeling for your teen a type of communication that is a prerequisite for healthy and fulfilling relationships. Assertiveness is a specific type of communication that will allow you to clearly state limits with your teen, ask for a change in his behavior, and give him feedback while increasing the likelihood of being heard.

Saying No

"Mom, can I use the car tonight to hang out with my friends? We're meeting at about midnight, so it shouldn't interfere with your plans." Annelisse, one of the parents I worked with years ago, received this request from her son, Timothy, as if it were the most natural thing for a teen to do, to hang out at midnight on a weekday with his friends. Teens, more often than not, make requests for money, clothes, birthday parties, trips, and all types of things, and often the parenting job is to say no. However, saying no becomes a tricky task when you suspect that your teen's emotional switch is going to turn on and a potential argument could start right away. Here are the steps to assertively say no to your teen when receiving inappropriate requests:

1. Verbally appreciate your teen's feelings when making a request.

2. Explain to your teen the rationale for saying no.

3. Offer choices to your teen.

Optional: if you don't have an immediate response, it is important to let your teen know that you will think about the request and get back to him after a certain period of time.

Did you notice that the first step for saying no is to appreciate your teen's feelings, wishes, and wants behind his request? The appreciating skills you learned in chapter 11 are key for developing assertive behaviors; they will certainly make room for your teen's needs to be seen at all times, even when he's making an inappropriate request. Imagine for a second how it would be for him to hear a radical no from you versus receiving an appreciative response. Quite different, right?

Here is an example of how Annelisse responded to Timothy's request: "Timothy, I can totally see how excited you are about hanging out with your friends, and it's really kind of you to think about how not to affect my regular schedule [appreciating verbally]. However, it's not safe to be walking around and driving in town at midnight, most places are closed, and it will be very stressful if something happens to you in the middle of the night [explaining the rationale]. What about if this weekend I drive you to your friend's home from 6:00 to 10:00 p.m. or maybe a sleepover at our house? [offering choices]."

Saying no in an assertive manner won't stop your teen from making all types of demands or requests, appropriate and inappropriate ones. However, learning from you, through firsthand experience, how to say no in a manner that doesn't damage the relationship between the two of you is a skill you're giving him in life. In the end, you're the emotional coach in your teen's life.

Making a Request

Let's think together about a scenario that I frequently encounter in my clinical work with teens: imagine that your teen has been cutting his wrists, using marijuana, drinking alcohol, and having random sexual encounters; at home, his bedroom is messy, clothes are all over the floor, and plates of food are left on the night table. What are your emotional reactions to these images? Notice the different types of thoughts that show up in your mind after holding those images. Any evaluative thought, future or past thoughts, any story about your teen, or even a rule broken by him? Did you notice any impulses to fix any or maybe all of those problems?

A regular day in the life of a teen suffering with intense emotional reactions is usually full of reactive behaviors, and it's challenging for any parent to navigate through those multiple problems. Chances are that solving any of these difficult situations involves making a request to your teen to adjust or change his behavior.

Pause for a moment and think about how often you ask your teen to start, stop, or do more or less of a specific behavior; quite likely, you have made these types of requests very often. Now, pause again and ask yourself how many of those requests end up in a conflict with your teen. Choosing what to address and assertively doing it will prevent things from going south with your teen. Asking for what you need is a skill that requires awareness, prioritization, and appropriate communication.

The secret ingredient for making requests from the beginning to the end is *behavioral clarity*, which means describing behaviors in a very observable manner and in a way that any person can watch the behavior happening step-by-step.

EXERCISE: Practicing Behavioral Clarify

Grab your parenting journal and write a list of your teen's problematic behaviors as specifically as possible. (Words like "laziness," "disengaged," and so on are not specific; a specific behavioral description is "throwing and leaving dirty clothes on the floor," "texting while having dinner," or "playing video games from 9:00 p.m. to 4:00 a.m.") Then organize these items into three problem categories: low, moderate, and high difficulty. Finally, based on the reorganization of the items, choose the least problematic ones to start practicing making requests. For example, after completing her list and organizing her items, Mayra decided to start working on her daughter Tessa's behavior of "throwing things in the trash even though the trash can is full and the garbage is spilling onto the floor."

Now here are the four elements that are fundamental when making a request:

1. Clearly state the problematic behavior as a description of the behavior. Quite often parents confuse descriptions with judgment thoughts. For instance, the thought *Janice is very lazy* is a judgment thought, but "Janice didn't brush her teeth after eating lunch" is a description of her behavior.

2. State your feelings about that particular behavior using *I-statements* so that you are not blaming your teen for your feelings. Making a comment such as "You make me so angry when…" is not helpful; instead, make sure to say "I feel angry when…" or "I feel sad when…" and so on when you are talking about how you feel in a situation.

3. State your thoughts about why this behavior is a problem for you. When you do this, avoid any criticism or generalizing

statements about who your teen is as a person because of this particular behavior. For instance, saying "When you leave your cup of coffee in the bathroom, I cannot stop thinking what a pig you have become" is different from saying "When you leave your cup of coffee in the bathroom, I get frustrated since I'm the one picking it up every morning while trying to get ready to leave the house."

4. Clearly state your request for a new behavior. Making your request for a new behavior needs to be very clearly stated, using words that describe a behavior that is observable. Saying things like "I would like you to be more organized and cleaner than before" won't help your teen to improve his behavior, because it's not a specific request. However, saying "I would like you to pick up the dirty clothes from the bathroom after taking a shower" is specific, and your teen will know exactly what you're asking from him.

When Mayra followed the above steps, she came up with the following request for Tessa: "Tessa, this morning I saw you throwing your breakfast leftovers into the full trashcan, and the garbage spilled onto the floor around it. I feel frustrated about it because it's important to me to keep the house clean for all of us and to avoid any bad odors or bugs coming into the house because of the trash on the floor. So, I need to ask you to please empty the bin when it is full."

When Mayra uses clarity as a guiding principle to make a request and follows all the suggested steps, she increases the chances to be heard by her daughter, decreases opportunities for escalation, because she's not accusing her teen of anything but is instead asserting herself, and teaches her teen how to make requests without damaging the relationship.

EXERCISE: Practicing Making Assertive Requests

See if you can come up with assertive requests, using the four fundamental elements for making a request, for the following scenarios:

1. Ask your teen to call if he will be home later than 10:00 p.m.

2. Ask your teen to come up with you to visit your parents this weekend.

3. Ask your teen to stop playing loud music after 9:00 p.m. on weekdays.

No relationship will survive if you don't express your concerns, disappointments, or requests. Making a request is a survival skill in the relationship with your teen, and it will allow you to address those rocky situations as they come up. Remember, not asking your teen for a change is prolonging more internal conflict for yourself.

Giving Feedback

It's quite likely that your teen's behavior is not going to be appropriate or helpful at all times, and as part of your parenting job description, you're the most suitable person to give him feedback. Giving feedback is different from making a request, because you're not asking your teen to change his behavior but simply letting him know your concerns, worries, and fears about a particular behavior or situation you observed. This is a very difficult task because dysregulated teens may perceive the feedback as personal criticism if their emotional switch is on.

At the same time, if you give your teen caring and effective feedback, you're teaching him how to handle the disagreements, concerns, worries, and differences that we all have in relationships. Giving feedback to your teen is very similar to the steps described when learning the skill of making a request, but with specific modifications:

1. Describe the behavior you're concerned about using I-statements.

2. State your feelings about it.

3. State your worry or concerned thoughts about it.

4. Offer your teen an invitation to talk about the behavior if he wants to and when he's ready to do so.

For instance, when Lizbeth practiced giving feedback to her son Philippe about dating multiple people, she told him, "Philippe, there is something I would like to share with you from a place of caring. I noticed that the last three weeks you have been going out with four different boys as your dates to different parties; I'm worried about this because I'm afraid you may get hurt or you may hurt other boys without wanting to do so. So let me know if you want to talk about it at some point. Your call. I'm here for you to figure things out together."

According to McKay, Davis, and Fanning (2009), there are three important principles for giving feedback: immediacy, honesty, and supportiveness.

Immediacy means giving feedback as soon as you see an inappropriate behavior or a potentially difficult situation for your teen. It's better to avoid giving feedback to your teen when he is with other teens or if there are relatives around.

Honesty refers to stating your real reaction, such as "It's hard for me. I found it challenging…"; it's not about making rude or tough statements but simply about saying why X behavior is difficult for you, keeping in mind that you are talking to a sensitive teen. Avoiding any sugarcoated statement, such as "It's really not a big deal," is highly recommended.

Supportiveness translates into doing the best you can to gently say what you need to say to your teen without making accusations about his character or blaming him for his faults. For example, statements like "You're too lazy" are not supportive; it's better to say "You didn't turn in your science homework this week."

Giving feedback is a core assertiveness skill that will allow you to state your concerns about your teen's behavior in a way that preserves the relationship and helps you exercise your parenting values.

Potential Blocks

As you might expect, when learning new skills and getting ready to put them into action, your mind will come up with all types of images, thoughts, or narratives, some of them helpful, some of them not. Again, a very important ACT skill is to notice your mind noise for what it is: mind noise. You cannot control what your mind comes up with, but you can certainly choose how to respond. For instance, when talking about assertiveness skills, a parent shared a thought that popped up for him in that moment: "Why do I have to explain myself or be so thoughtful when talking to my teen, when I'm the parent?" Are you having a similar thought or some version of it? If so, let's briefly take a look at what this thought does for you.

EXERCISE: Looking at What Mind Noise Does for You

Pick up your parenting journal and answer these three questions:

1. What do you want to call those types of thoughts that your mind is coming up with?

2. If you go along with those thoughts and do what they dictate, what happens in the short term and in the long term to the relationship with your teen?

3. If those thoughts dictate your behavior, does it help you be the parent you want to be?

For instance, when Annelisse answered those questions she came up with the responses below:

1. "I called those thoughts 'my why thoughts.'"

2. "When I offer no explanations to Timothy, but instead insist that he does what I say, he usually fights back and we argue more in the moment; that's my short-term consequence. In the long-term, we both get resentful and angry with each other."

3. "Using an angry tone of voice, yelling, or even firmly repeating myself, I am far from the understanding and supportive mother I want to be; my demanding behavior is usually masking my own frustration. But in the moment, it's really hard to see this, because it happens very quickly."

Annelisse acknowledged that it's easier to ask her teen to do X in a given moment than to notice the frustration, exhaustion, and even powerlessness she feels at times as a mother.

Our minds play tricks, and it's natural that when incorporating assertive behaviors, your mind is going to be like a popcorn machine and will throw at you all types of thoughts; your mind is just doing its job. Then here is a key ACT question: would you be willing to have those uncomfortable thoughts and still follow through with the suggested steps when saying no, making a request to your teen, or giving feedback, so you can be the parent you want to be? The choice is yours.

Summary and Looking Ahead

Successful relationships are partly based on how we handle our internal reactions and partly based on how we handle our behaviors with others. By practicing how to say no, making assertive requests, and giving caring feedback to your teen, you are teaching him the core skills of an effective communicator and increasing the chances of him creating healthy relationships. No healthy and successful relationship comes premade into our interpersonal world; each one of them requires a style of communication that facilitates understanding of one another and the fulfillment of our emotional needs.

Now let's face it: even if you give assertiveness skills your best shot when communicating with your teen, conflict is going to show up sooner or later. Some of the issues you argue about may be fleeting ones compared to other times when you and your teen may argue about the same issues over and over. You're going to need a different set of skills to handle these repetitive problematic behaviors, so you can stop nagging and start rewarding your teen. Ready to learn how?

CHAPTER 13

"Stop Nagging, Start Rewarding": Behavioral-Management Skills

Have you ever noticed your mind having the thought *Why do I keep saying the same thing over and over, and my teen still behaves the same way?* Or maybe at a random time, you find your mind comes up with image after image of all the times you had the same argument with your teen? This chapter is about figuring out why your teen keeps doing the same thing over and over despite your asking her not to do so, nagging her, and even scolding her.

A Behavioral Framework for Your Teen's Behavior

Within ACT, human behavior refers to everything a person does, feels, senses, and thinks within a given context. Your teen, as any human being, continues to do a behavior because something keeps the behavior going, or in behavioral terms, because something reinforces the behavior. Learning to use a behavioral framework to understand your teen's behavior is like learning to wear a pair of glasses to understand what keeps your teen's challenging behaviors going and what happens behaviorally between the two of you in a moment of conflict.

There are two concepts that you need to be pretty clear about: *context* and *consequences*.

You cannot understand your teen's behaviors and your own without understanding the context in which they occur. By context,

I'm referring to a specific situation in which a problematic behavior takes place. Every time we do something, there is a natural consequence for that behavior, whether we're aware of it or not, that could either increase or decrease it the next time it gets triggered. Now here is what's interesting to keep in mind. If the behavior in consideration increases or is augmented, it's because the consequences acted as *reinforcers*. Reinforcers can be either positive, if you add something pleasurable, or negative, if you remove something aversive.

If the behavior in consideration decreases or is minimized, it's because the consequences acted as *punishers*. Punishers can be either positive, if you add something aversive, or negative, if you remove something pleasurable.

Using this behavioral framework when explaining your teen's behaviors, we could say that her behaviors are reinforced when you add something she likes or remove something she dislikes, and other behaviors are decreased, or are punished, because you add something she doesn't like or you remove something she likes. Now, because of our upbringing, socialization, and the tricks that our mind plays with us, the words "punishers," "positive," and "negative" may have different connotations. But behaviorally speaking, the word "punisher" is simply a descriptor of whether a behavior has decreased or not, and "positive" and "negative" basically mean that you either add or remove something after a behavior has occurred.

Putting all these behavioral terms together, you can see how they can explain your teen's behavior:

	Positive	Negative
Reinforcer or augmenter (increases a behavior)	Adding something your teen likes	Removing something your teen doesn't like
Punisher or minimizer (decreases a behavior)	Adding something your teen doesn't like	Removing something your teen likes

How do reinforcers and punishers apply to your relationship with your teen's behavior? To make it easier, we'll refer to reinforcers as *augmenters* and punishers as *minimizers*. Let's imagine that your teen comes home and tells you, "I'm feeling really sad because no one friended me on Facebook this week." Your response could be, "I'm sorry, that's hard to hear when I know you have been making an effort to connect with people." In response, your teen feels heard and understood. In this example, it is safe to say that your response (an augmenter) has increased the likelihood that your teen will continue to tell you how she's feeling.

Now, let's imagine the same scenario, but this time you tell your teen, "That doesn't make sense. You don't need to feel down if no one friended you on Facebook. Besides, who cares about Facebook? You already have a lot of friends in your class." In response, your teen feels unheard and quickly gets upset. Therefore, the likelihood of your teen sharing again her feelings with you has decreased because of your response (a positive minimizer: your behavior added an uncomfortable emotion for your teen, unappreciation).

Let's take these behavioral terms one step further and see how they operate together when arguing with your teen. The scenario below puts together all these concepts by looking at what happens before (antecedent), your specific parenting response (the behavior to analyze), and what happens after that behavior occurs (consequences).

Context: Sean (parent) and Sylvia (teen) are discussing plans for the weekend at the breakfast table.

Antecedent (what happens before to you and your teen): Sean suggests they go to a movie together. Sylvia screams, "But I told you I want to go to Jim's [Sylvia's boyfriend]!"

Sean is feeling angry about being screamed at by his daughter and thinks, *This is outrageous. She's so disrespectful.*

Parenting behavior: Sean yells at Sylvia as loudly as he can: "You're grounded for one month, no TV, no hanging out with friends, and you come directly home from school every day, no exceptions."

Consequence (what happens after to you and to your teen):
Sean feels energized after screaming (augmenter).

Sylvia feels upset and yells back at Sean, "I hate you when you treat me like this! You're the worst father ever. I don't care what you think I should do. I won't do it anyway."

Notice that after Sean screamed back at his daughter, the immediate consequence for him was an energizing feeling, which is a positive augmenter because it's quite likely that he will scream again to experience that energizing feeling. Now the challenge is that Sean's screaming behavior (augmenter) had an impact on his daughter's behavior, because she ended up screaming back at him. So now you can see how Sean's behavior had a direct impact on his daughter's response to him without Sean even realizing it.

Now let's consider a different response in a similar context with this father and daughter:

Context: Sean and Sylvia are discussing plans for the weekend at breakfast. Sean suggests they watch a movie or maybe play video games together.

Antecedent (what happens before to you and your teen): Sylvia quickly says to Sean, "Dad, you don't understand: I need to see Jim [boyfriend]; otherwise I'll wind up thinking about suicide. Is that what you want for me? Do you want me to keep thinking about suicide over and over, and then you find your daughter dead?"

Sean feels scared about losing his daughter and also frustrated. He has the thought *Here it is again, the suicidal threat.*

Parenting behavior: Sean tells his daughter, "Sweetie, I know how much you value your time with Jim, and I'm glad you find that being with him helps to handle your thoughts about suicide. However, when I hear you telling me how hard it is for you not to think about suicide, it makes me think that even though you seem to be doing well in other respects, we may have to consider hospitalization. I'm wondering if it is possible to find other ways to handle those sad feelings beyond spending the entire weekend with your boyfriend, so I don't have to worry about you thinking about suicide or the need for hospitalization."

Consequence (what happens afterward to you and your teen): Sylvia pauses and then responds to her dad, "Dad I don't want to go to any hospital or inpatient program. You know that I hate going to those places. They make everything worse for me. The only thing that helps is when I'm with Jim."

Sean feels proud of himself for how he handled the situation and relieved to not hear Sylvia insist that she will commit suicide, but instead talk about wanting to visit her boyfriend.

In this example, it is understood that Sean and Sylvia have previously fully discussed these types of statements in therapy, and Sylvia's safety has been properly assessed by a mental health professional; however, Sylvia, like many teens struggling with emotion dysregulation, is quick to act on her emotions and doesn't see any options besides thinking about suicide in that moment as the only way to handle the situation.

Sylvia's mind may be hooked to the thought *Hanging out with my boyfriend is the only way to manage my depressive thoughts; if I can't spend time with him, then I will likely contemplate suicide.* Sean experiences frustration and fear when he hears these statements but recognizes the impact of reacting to them on Sylvia's behavior. With caring and compassion, he is able to respond to his daughter while still setting a limit.

The outcome is that Sylvia doesn't make those suicidal comments threats again, and Sean experiences some relief when she doesn't continue to make them; he also feels proud of how he handled the situation. Although Sylvia continued to insist on visiting her boyfriend for the weekend, that's a more manageable behavior for Sean than her suicidal threats.

It is extremely important to be clear about identifying what happens after a problematic behavior, because your parenting response may simply be reinforcing a problematic behavior without your realizing it. As you can see, context, workability, and consequences are extremely important in looking at how your parenting responses, not only in moments of conflict but at all times, have an impact on your teen's actions.

EXERCISE: Looking at Your Parenting Response

Moving forward and incorporating behavioral management into your parenting repertoire, do this exercise at the end of the day: grab your parenting journal, think about an argument you had with your teen, write down the antecedents, your parenting response, and the consequences, and finally see whether your parenting response is increasing or decreasing your teen's problematic behavior. Which behavior are you reinforcing in a given moment?

One Extra Tip: Behavioral Consistency

The timing in which an augmenter or minimizer is delivered is extremely important for managing your teen's behaviors; this is called a *consequence schedule*. A consequence schedule can be consistent or intermittent.

A consequence schedule is *consistent* when you deliver an augmenter or minimizer after your teen engages in a particular behavior, which is ideal and recommended. If there is inconsistency or irregularity when delivering consequences, then you're creating what is called *intermittent reinforcement*. Intermittent reinforcement will simply makes things worse for you and your teen, because she won't ever know if her behavior will be followed by a minimizer or augmenter, and therefore, sometimes she may engage in appropriate behaviors and other times she will do whatever her emotions push her to do. Here is an example of intermittent: checking your email or Facebook page, sometimes you will receive an email or there will be a new post, and sometimes nothing new will show up; because you never know when to expect what, you continue checking your email and Facebook more and more often.

Let's apply what you learned in this chapter by putting all these concepts together in a behavioral plan to address your teen's challenging behaviors.

Creating Fun Behavioral Plans

Behavioral plans are just plans to address your teen's challenging behaviors: adding or removing things your teen likes or dislikes, so you can either increase or decrease the likelihood of a specific behavior happening. Traditional parenting models have used behavioral plans as a very authoritarian tool to address the teen's problematic behaviors; the challenge with those traditional approaches is that the more you force a behavior without making the teen part of the plan, the less she will comply with it, and the final outcome is simply more conflict in your household. Because ACT is all about creating behavioral flexibility between you and your teen, a behavioral plan is a dynamic process between the two of you rather than an authoritarian road map or a dry prescription of your teen's behaviors. Creating behavioral plans will certainly help you be a top-notch parent, and believe it or not, it can also be fun to create them with your teen.

Let me share an example of a behavioral plan of one of the families I was working with years ago. After discussing the target behaviors with their teen, including the specific augmenters and minimizers, they decided to follow their teen's suggestion that a consequence for him not completing his homework three out of five nights a week would be writing a five-page essay about "how important it is to spend money against gay rights." This was a positive minimizer because, in the context of this teen's life, he was gay and a strong advocator for gay rights, so for him to have to write an essay against his beliefs would certainly be an aversive experience that would make him think twice about not completing his homework. This example may give you a sense of how behavioral plans can be created from thinking outside of the box and how the family can engage in this process instead of it being a micromanaging tool to keep track of the teen's behavior.

Here are the principles to keep in mind when developing a behavioral plan:

1. The purpose of a behavioral plan is to create golden opportunities for you and your teen to engage in more helpful conversations instead of arguing over and over about a specific matter. Discuss this specific goal with your teen transparently and from a teaching place (not a punitive one).

135

2. Watch out for your mind coming up with judgmental thoughts, future- or past-oriented thoughts, or stories about yourself or your teen.

3. Put together with your teen a list of problematic behaviors that are behaviorally observable. For instance, writing down a problematic behavior as "disrespectful behavior" is too vague and not easily identifiable for both of you. Stating things like "using a soft tone of voice when making a request" or "asking Dad for a ride to the mall twenty-four hours in advance" are observable behaviors.

4. Select with your teen three specific problematic behaviors to work on. When you're starting something new, it's best to start with a problem that is not extremely difficult, so you and your teen start mastering a skill together step-by-step instead of getting frustrated with it right away.

5. Create with your teen an inventory of five *likes* (augmenters) and five *dislikes* (minimizers) for the three problematic behaviors you will start working on. You can even be creative and put together a list of "likes" and "dislikes" in a menu format as if you were going to a restaurant. Here is an extra tip for you: watch out for harsh punishers such as "no Facebook for three months" or "no hanging out with friends for a month." Those minimizers are very intense and disproportionate to the social context and developmental mind of your teen. As you know, the concept of time is very different for adults and for teens. These kinds of punishers are like telling your teen that she has to wait an eternity before being able to use Facebook again.

6. Create a chart with this behavioral plan and make sure that all behaviors are checked on a daily basis to start; please discuss with your teen what time of day both of you will go over the chart.

7. Do your best to be consistent and consistent again!

Instead of nagging, scolding, or arguing for hours with your teen about the same thing, following through with all of the above steps will help you have a solid, fun, and effective behavioral plan to address specific problematic behaviors. Moving forward, say no to nagging and yes to more enjoying each other's company.

Watch Out, Thoughts!

As you can expect, your mind will come up with all types of thoughts when getting ready to implement your behavioral plan. If your mind is having the "nothing is going to work" thoughts like *Why do I have to do all this? Nothing is going to change in my house*, then answer the following questions:

1. Are the "nothing is going to work" thoughts the ones that continually show up in your mind when taking steps toward change?

2. What are the short- and the long-term effects of following these thoughts and taking action on them in the relationship with your teen?

3. If you act on these "nothing is going to work" thoughts, does the relationship with your teen get better or worse?

Using behavioral-management skills is not an easy task, especially when you're raising a teen struggling with emotional sensitivity, but it's not an impossible one either. Sometimes it's natural to become a lenient or an authoritarian parent, but is that the type of parent that you really want to be? Are permissiveness or bossiness your true parenting values?

Summary and Looking Ahead

Here is the take-home message: addressing your teen's problematic repetitive behaviors with common strategies, such as talking over and over about it, punishing her multiple times, reminding her fifty times about how she's supposed to behave, shouting at her, using eye-rolling, or even giving her the silent treatment, will simply perpetuate the cycle of conflict and an ongoing disconnection from each other. You are both hurting, not just you, not just her. Behavioral-management skills are the alternative skills to nagging, scolding, and arguing over and over with your teen.

Looking at the context, the antecedents, your parenting behavior, and the consequences when dealing with those rocky situations will allow you to see whether your responses are effective or not. When wondering about the workability of your parenting response, ask yourself, *Is my behavior helping me to walk toward or away from the parent I want to be?*

Our life, as it occurs in the real world, is full of natural consequences, reinforcers and punishers, or as we refer to them in this chapter, augmenters or minimizers. Everything we do, say, or feel has a consequence. For example, if we don't go to work, there is a consequence; if your teen fails to turn in a paper, there is a consequence. Effective parenting is about preparing your teen to face life as it occurs. Naturally, as a parent, you want to protect your teen from any painful situation; however, if your behaviors are overprotective or inconsistent, you're not preparing your teen to face life as it happens, with pleasant and not-so-pleasant consequences; your teen will quickly learn that it's okay to behave however she wants, and that consequences or rules are for others, not for her.

Remember that consistency is vital in learning any skill but especially when learning to use behavioral-management skills. Intermittent reinforcement, because of its unpredictability, makes it really hard for anyone, not just your teen, to change a behavior.

Finally, keep in mind that behavioral plans can be fun, and you really need to create them with your teen, as a team, not just you in the middle of the night or in the middle of a fight with your teen. You don't have control over your teen's behavior, but you can choose how to respond to it. Your call.

CHAPTER 14

"Let's Deal with This": Conflict Resolution Skills

After a parent coaching session, Louise and Jonathan left with a specific plan about how to respond to their son Benjamin's suicidal threats. We laid out specific responses and even anticipated internal barriers: future-oriented thoughts and intense feelings of hopelessness. They returned the following week, and Louise recounted what happened at home: "I lost it; I couldn't take it anymore, and the next thing I knew, I started screaming at Benjamin and telling him how inconsiderate and disrespectful he is by threatening us with suicide. I simply lost it. He kept screaming in my face that if I didn't let him go back to his old school with his old friends, it would be my fault if he died. I was so upset that after screaming at him and bursting into tears, all I could think of was a shot of Scotch, and it was eight-thirty in the morning!"

The situation presented above is a common one for parents: you have a very well-thought-out plan about how to handle your teen's behavior, but when you are in the middle of this sticky situation with him, things escalate, and suddenly you find yourself using the old strategies that didn't work before. You didn't make choices in those moments; your automatic pilot just went on. You're definitely not the only one; most parents go through similar situations. Learning to handle your teen's argumentativeness will not only have positive consequences for your relationship but also be a gift you are giving to him. Who is better than you to teach him how to handle conflict in relationships?

Relationships Are Complex

Relationships are complex by nature. We all search for connection, and we all want to be seen, accepted, and loved for who we are; however, sooner or later there will be conflict. Conflict is a vulnerable moment for the people involved in it, and it can be a source of discomfort and separation or a source of greater connection and growth. The thought of a conflict-free relationship is certainly a myth, and the relationship with your teen is no exception.

The most common arguments I've observed parents encounter with their teens happen when saying no, making a request for a change in their behavior, or needing to give their teen feedback about a particular situation. All of these scenarios were covered in chapter 12 on assertiveness skills, but naturally each one of these situations is also a possibility for a conflict with your teen.

Regardless of how difficult it may seem to handle conflict with your teen or how unreasonable your teen's arguments are, he still needs to learn conflict-resolution skills. You, like most parents, go through all types of internal reactions in those sensitive moments. Are you willing to learn to handle your own internal reactions while teaching your teen how to handle conflict without damaging your relationship with him? If so, the next section will take a look into the most common conflict-management strategies that parents use.

Tricky Thoughts When Solving a Conflict

Most of the parents I work with when dealing with conflict with their teens may be fused with some version of the thought *I'm the parent, and I'm right*. Can you pause and check in with yourself if that's a thought you get hooked on when dealing with problems with your teen? If so, what happens when you act on that thought? What do you do in the middle of a conflict with him?

Over the years, I have noticed how the "I'm right, and I'm the parent" thought usually drives an authoritarian parenting approach. Authoritarian parenting behaviors for handling your teen's argumentativeness frequently come with aversive conflict-management strategies, such as blaming, name-calling or making generalizations, or making threats or ultimatums. These strategies may work to stop your teen's behavior in the short term, but they model ineffective, unhelpful, and potentially damaging ways to handle conflict. No one likes to be shut down with restrictive rules of behavior just because someone tells us to do so. Do you remember a time when you may have used one or all of these strategies? Can you recall the outcome in the moment and later on for you?

Unfortunately, the more that you rely on these aversive strategies, the more that you and your teen are simply rehearsing how to use an imposition of your needs on each other as a way to handle interpersonal conflict. Your teen will learn new and healthy responses based on the experience of the two of you resolving conflict. The question remains: who better than you to teach these skills to your teen?

Creating a Framework for Handling Conflict

Here is your task as parent: to teach your teen how to deal with fights in a way that preserves a relationship he cares for. How to do it? You create a framework for the two of you to discuss a conflict. Creating a framework for handling conflict involves the following microsteps:

1. Specify a time for the two of you to talk.

2. Describe a problem to talk about, behaviorally speaking.

3. Stick only to discussing that problem.

4. Agree that name-calling, blaming, threats, or any other aversive response is off-limits during the conversation.

Both of you may struggle when implementing this new framework to handle disagreements, which goes along with learning a new skill, but what's the alternative: to go back to old aversive strategies? You may have the urge to do so, and if you were to do so, what would be the outcome for the relationship with your teen? If you were to use this new framework for handling conflict, what could be the outcome?

Here is an important tip: if any of these aversive strategies are present—name-calling, blaming, or threatening—it is very important that you name that behavior, let your teen know about it, and disengage from the conversation. Disengaging from the conflict doesn't mean that you and your teen won't ever talk about it; it only means that you both will pause for a given amount of time and then start again.

Within ACT, you are asked to choose the parent you want to be at all times, even when you're in the middle of an emotional battle with your teen; this is one of the most challenging tasks you have as a parent but not an unachievable one. It's challenging, because your teen has said or done something upsetting, not once but numerous times, and it really hurts. And even when you're in the midst of the conflict, it's still a moment to pause and really ask yourself what type of parent you want to be in that precise moment: a reactive one or an effective one. Reactive parents handle the conflict by allowing themselves to be driven by the emotion, the anger, and the hurt; effective parents pause and choose how to respond. If you want to respond effectively to conflict, here is the first thing you need to do: go back to your breathing!

Breathing Comes First

Breathing is one of the most basic life functions and is extremely useful when handling conflict because it brings you right back into the moment. Breathing, when intentionally practiced, activates a particular part of our nervous system, called the parasympathetic nervous system, that regulates our relaxation response and activates our soothing system, which in turns activates frontal lobe activity in the brain, so we can think better. For instance, when people pray, their parasympathetic nervous system is activated, and therefore they experience a sense of relaxation. The more relaxed and soothed we are, the better we can think. Here is a tip: if you want to maximize the benefits of your breathing and really wake up your parasympathetic nervous system and frontal lobe, your exhalation needs to be intentionally longer than your inhalation. Here is what to do to start practicing a focused breathing:

1. Place one hand on your stomach.

2. Start inhaling while counting from one to three.

3. When breathing out, count from one to seven.

Practicing this breathing will help you to feel grounded and to slow down before and during a heated conversation with your teen. If you're into using apps, you can even use one of them to get in the habit of practicing your breathing and monitoring the quality of it. Here's the deal: every time your teen starts an argument with you because you say no, or every time you emphatically confront him about a particular behavior or address a repetitive problematic behavior, you are invited to make an extra effort and practice your breathing in that precise moment.

Handling Your Teen's Argumentativeness

Even if you assertively say no to your teen or assertively make a request, it's quite likely that your teen will argue back with you. Are you surprised? Arguing back is typical teen behavior, but managing a denial of their wishes is a bit more difficult for teens struggling with emotional vulnerability because their emotions overwhelm them in the moment; when their emotional switch goes on, you may hear complaints such as, "You just don't get me," "You don't understand me," "I'm a prisoner of this house," or "Why do I have to do everything that you want me to do?"

Learning to pause and choose your parenting response in the middle of an argument is a core skill. I can tell you by direct experience that it has made a huge difference in my life to pause, step back, and ask myself what type person I want to be in the middle of a conflict instead of giving into anger, yelling, or demanding others to change or do what I believe needs to be done.

Reactivity and its cousin anger are invigorating emotions in the moment because they keep us on fire, but later on, the embarrassment and the shame kick in harder. Pausing and choosing to not lash out, scream back, attack back, or make sarcastic comments takes a lot of effort, and it is priceless to notice at the end of the conflict that you gave your best to de-escalate the situation, even if the person in front of you doesn't see it that way.

Here is the main invitation to you when handling conflict with your teen: turn up your ACT skills all the way. By "all the way," I mean give it your best shot when using each one of them. Let's look at them all at a glance:

- Breathe slowly intentionally.

- Make a commitment with yourself.

- Turn up your defusion-skills dial.

- Turn up your appreciation-skills dial.

- Notice verbal distractions.

- Make your assertive statement.

- Get out of talking in circles.

Now that you have a sense of all these skills, let's go over each one of them.

Breathe slowly intentionally. You are highly encouraged to intentionally slow down your breathing as soon as you see a conflict starting with your teen; again, by breathing slowly you are activating the part of your nervous system that allows you to be present in the moment.

Make a commitment with yourself. When the conflict with your teen starts, you're facing a moment of choice to either behave based on your parenting values or go back to old behaviors. No one can make this decision for you. Old unworkable behaviors fight for survival and can get quickly activated. New values-based behaviors feel uneasy at the beginning, but the more you practice them, the more natural they become, and they can substantially improve the moments of conflict with your teen.

Turn up your defusion-skills dial. When your teen is upset and making all types of comments, requests, and even demands about a situation, it's natural that your judgment machine or the master author of your mind gets activated, and there is no need to deny, change, or get hooked on those thoughts. Instead, acknowledge them, name them for what they are, and then check with yourself if those judgments, past or future thoughts, or narratives about your teen are helpful or not in the midst of a conflict. Cindy, a former client of mine, named those thoughts as "Judge Cindy" when they were showing up in her mind; she recognized them right away because of their harsh voice. If you defuse from those thoughts and hold them lightly, you give yourself a chance to choose a response to that conflict, based on your parenting values and not on the heat of the situation.

Turn up your appreciation-skills dial. Can you recognize your teen's difficulty when you ask for a change of his behavior or he listens to a no from you? Because your teen struggles with emotional sensitivity, his capacity to experience emotions is already amplified, and therefore it's extremely important to let him know that you see and understand his struggle, even if you disagree with it. A large dosage of verbal appreciation could significantly de-escalate the conflict between the two of you.

Notice verbal distractions. A verbal distraction is any comment your teen may make in the middle of the conflict that takes you both away from choosing alternative behaviors. Common verbal distractions that teens may engage in include comments either about the past (such as "You always do this" or "You said the same thing last week") or about the future (such as "This is never going to stop" or "You won't ever get me"). If your teen makes comments that are verbal distractions, make sure you bring him back to the present by gently saying "Let's go back to talking about the issue here."

Make your assertive statement. Whether you are saying no, making a request, or giving feedback to your teen, all you can do is say it again while making sure that you're not responding to any verbally distracting comments he's making. Saying the same assertive statement over again may feel like you're a broken record, but here's the deal: you're teaching your teen to solve one thing at a time, and this is what effective conflict management is about.

145

Get out of talking in circles. If you find yourself repeating the same assertive statements or your teen continues to rely on verbal distractions, then you can acknowledge that you both are arguing or are talking in circles, by telling your teen, "We're getting nowhere right now. Let's take a break from this, and we can talk about it either later today or tomorrow."

Although handling conflict is a challenging task, especially with your highly sensitive teen, it's not impossible. Putting together and practicing all these skills will help you handle arguments and fights with him.

Summary and Looking Ahead

The wish for a conflict-free home is just that, a wishful thought. In this chapter, you have been invited to create a framework for you and your teen to handle disagreements in a very healthy manner by turning off all types of blaming, name-calling, and threat making. You have also been reminded that breathing is not only a basic function of our body but also a core skill when dealing with conflict, because a longer exhalation will activate the parasympathetic nervous system and invite your body to calm down as a whole. Six specific steps were covered for handling your teen's argumentativeness; none of those steps are doable unless you make a commitment to your parenting values and do your best to de-escalate the conflict with your teen.

Conflict is a sensitive moment for you and your teen, but ACT skills can help you make it a moment of growth and connection. Your teen can learn these foundational skills by directly experiencing them with you.

For this coming week, recall a past situation in which you said no to your teen and he argued about it. Then grab your parenting journal and write down the steps for handling conflict, including specific actions you could have taken for every step. This practice may feel irrelevant or artificial, and your mind may be saying *So much work. It doesn't make sense.* Then, here is a question for you: are you willing to have those thoughts and still write down the responses to handling conflict with your teen because it helps you to be the parent you want to be?

Handling conflict is not an easy parenting task when dealing with a highly sensitive teen, and at times anger may show up. So, let's be prepared for it by learning some anger skills.

CHAPTER 15

"Taming the Demon": Anger Skills

Up to this point, by reading and practicing the skills taught in this book, you have learned a bunch of ACT skills, such as mindfulness, appreciation, empathy, assertiveness, behavioral management, and conflict resolution. "So far, so good." It all sounds manageable on paper, but it's quite likely that using these skills initially felt like a new shoe you were breaking in, uncomfortable, and even when you try your best, you don't know how your teen will respond. When parents are giving their best and their teen does not respond as they wish, they understandably get angry. This chapter is all about helping you to face those moments when things go wrong, terribly wrong with your teen, and you're angry or very angry.

We all have had angry moments because someone has hurt us, intentionally or unintentionally. As a parent, you may be able to write a full book about the many instances in which your teen has done or said something that really pushed your limits and, without realizing it, you may have yelled, screamed, threatened with punishment, and said all types of nasty things you later regretted. Sometimes, on reflection, you found your angry response justified; other times, you found yourself feeling embarrassed by your response and not knowing how to undo all your behaviors.

Among the wide range of emotions we experience, anger is one of the most complex ones, because in the moment we start feeling angry, we also start feeling empowered and energized to the point that we don't realize how quickly our emotions are intensifying; we can easily be controlled by anger and act on it. It's as if with anger, like the Hulk, you may turn into something unrecognizable and destructive, even if in the moment you may feel powerful and even believe that acting on anger is the right thing to do.

The topic of anger has occupied the bookshelves of libraries and bookstores over the years, and it's quite likely that some of these books still maintain old myths about anger. Let's go over them instead of being radically hooked on or fused with them.

Myths About Anger Applied to Parenting

We cannot move forward without revisiting at least the most popular myths that apply to parenting teens. You may be familiar with some of these myths, but still I invite you to read this section since it could be a good reminder for you about all the misconceptions on anger.

Myth: "My Anger Is My Teen's Fault"

Most of the parents I work with sooner or later make comments such as "It's my teen's fault, she makes me so angry" or "If he didn't do what he did, I wouldn't be so mad." This is a common response, but here is the caveat: your teen's behaviors may be the catalyst of your anger, as my dear friend Sean says, but the only owner of those angry thoughts and feelings and how to handle them is you, not your teen. Your teen's behaviors are upsetting to you and only you; otherwise everyone would be upset by what your teen does. Others hear the same words, see the same situation, and yet they are not carried away by anger. You get upset at what your teen does or says because there is something unique to you and within you. Making sense of your angry reactions is natural, because you're hurting, but blaming your teen for how you respond to your anger is avoiding accountability for your behavior, and it denies you the opportunity to take effective action as the parent you want to be.

Myth: "Anger Is the Only Way I Can Manage My Teen's Behavior"

Because being a parent 24/7 of a sensitive teen is hard work, it's natural that you may have learned to use anger as a strategy to manage your teen's challenging behavior, and because it works to stop your teen from saying or doing something upsetting, you have learned to rely on anger to control your teen's behavior. It's as if you've learned to dance with a particular routine, and because you have rehearsed it over and over, it becomes natural to dance using that routine.

The challenge is that the more you use anger to handle your teen's behavior, the more you are getting fused with thoughts along the lines of *Getting angry is the only way to handle her behavior* without looking at whether it's helpful or not to the relationship with her. As you have been reading in this book, when a situation is very upsetting, there are clearly other skills you could apply to handle your teen's behavior and the intensity of your own emotions that are more conducive toward the parent you want to be.

Myth: "Anger Is Always Helpful When Dealing with My Teen"

Another popular myth about anger is that experiencing anger is always helpful and healthy, because it tells you that something is wrong. However, as you may have already discovered while reading this book, nothing is simply always good or always bad. At times, anger acts as a red light that alerts us that something is not working for us in a particular situation. Other times, when you are taken over by the urge to be the one who says the last word, to win in the situation, or when you are moved to make sarcastic or derogatory comments to your teen, anger may be unhelpful and damaging to your relationship. Distinguishing anger as a warning signal from aggressive anger is extremely important when dealing with your teen.

Myth: "Venting Anger About My Teen Is Healthy"

If you have read any book on anger in the past, you may be familiar with the myth that venting anger is healthy. This myth stems from the work of Sigmund Freud and his followers supporting the notions that bottling up anger is unhealthy and unexpressed anger needs to be released in a cathartic manner. The work of Carol Tavris (1989) clearly disproved the notion that venting or releasing anger when slamming a door, punching a pillow, or screaming loudly will make things better; in fact, in her research she demonstrated that venting anger will simply make you more upset. Blowing off steam is simply not beneficial for your mind or body, and it will not help your relationships. Screaming, yelling, or insulting a person doesn't help with solving a conflict; quite the opposite, it simply makes the situation worse. Those behaviors don't reduce anger even a little; they actually increase it.

EXERCISE: Defusing from Angry Myths

Now that we have covered the most common misconceptions about anger in regard to parenting, and just in case your mind continues to hold on to one or all of them as absolute truth, see if you can practice defusion when these myths show up in your mind. Here is a defusion exercise to carry out: imagine that your mind is like a local newspaper, and like any newspaper, it has a political bias and tries to catch your attention with sensational headlines; while you're flipping over the newspaper, you see all those myths about anger printed in bold and capital letters as headlines are, you notice them, you read them, and you continue flipping the newspaper without doing anything, just noticing them.

If you get angry not only with your teen but also in other relationships, meaning that anger happens too often, too much, and for too long, you may be dealing with chronic anger problems. If this is the case, you are going to require extra skills to tame this demon. As with every other aspect of your relationship with your teen that this book covers, work on this only if you're ready and sincerely want to. I would highly recommend the book *ACT on Life Not on Anger* by Eifert, McKay, and Forsyth (2006).

Not Letting Anger Control You

Anger is an unavoidable emotion that colors all relationships, including the relationship with your teen. I'm not telling you that you shouldn't feel angry, frustrated, or even resentful toward your teen; your angry feelings are very real. But if anger controls you, there will be no opportunity for you to choose to behave as the parent you want to be, decrease the conflict with your teen, and fundamentally improve the relationship with her.

The parents I work with often tell me, "But my teen is so angry toward me, he's so aggressive, that there is no way for me not to be angry as well." It's understandable, and I get it. It does make sense that you get angry, that you are fused with the thought *If they're angry, of course, I'm angry too.* But responding to anger with anger is like having a positively charged ion contacting another positive charged ion: they will naturally repel each other. Responding to anger with anger leaves you and your teen poles apart from each other until you both lose connection. If you pause for a second, notice your experience: how did it go when your teen was angry and you got angry as well? Was that a helpful interaction for your relationship with her?

Quite likely anger has worked in the short term in the middle of an argument with your teen, but in the long run, it maybe simply eliminate any possibility of creating a fulfilling and healthy relationship with her. If you want to make a shift and handle anger in a nondestructive manner, there are two important ACT concepts to keep in mind when thinking about anger: account-ability and response-ability.

Account-Ability and Response-Ability

Being *account-able* means that despite being exposed to anger triggers in a particular situation with your teen, you acknowledge that you are 100 percent accountable for your behavior. It's not your teen's fault that you behave the way you do when feeling angry.

Response-ability is recognizing that when experiencing anger during interactions with your teen, you can still choose how to respond to her behavior as an effective parent and not as a reactive one. You cannot choose whether you feel angry or not, but you can decide what to do with that anger. This decision is a personal choice to make. Usually, when I share the idea of practicing response-ability during parent coaching sessions, I hear fused responses, such as "There is no way I can stop screaming. When I lose it, I lose it." In a moment of anger, it seems like a colossal task to pause, step back, and choose your responses, but if you're willing to make a shift from reactive parenting to values-based parenting, the next pages will show you how to do it.

EXERCISE: From Furious to Curious

For the next couple of moments, look at your angry behaviors from a place of curiosity, like an archeologist discovering a fossil for first time. To start, let's identify those *anger hazards* that are part of your daily life with your teen. Pick up your parenting journal and see if you can make a list of those situations you encounter with your teen that trigger anger over and over. For instance, Susan identified the following anger hazards when thinking about her son Lou:

"Not completing homework on time."

"Megahours of texting his friends while having a family gathering."

"Hiding cigarettes in his bedroom despite being forbidden to smoke."

"Posting on Facebook how much he hates living with his parents."

Now, after reading your anger hazard list, choose a particular anger hazard to work on for this exercise. Because this is the first time you're practicing this type of exercise, it's better if you choose a scene that is mildly upsetting. When you're ready, do your best to recall and hold the image of this upsetting memory in your mind for a couple of minutes, as if you're really discovering and exploring it for first time. Give yourself some time, noticing all the aspects of that angry situation in your mind. Then, answer the following questions in your parenting journal:

1. What were the emotions that came up for you just before or alongside the anger? (Naturally, you may want to say "just anger," but do the best you can to look again and see if there was any other feeling next to the anger or before the anger arose.)

2. Ask yourself, *What button was pushed in me? Why does it make me so upset? Why does my teen's behavior irritate me so much?*

3. What are those angry thoughts showing up? Any judgment thoughts about your teen? Any expectations or rules? Any future-oriented thoughts? Did you notice any narrative about who your teen is?

4. Did you notice any sensation or body reaction in that moment? Any type of discomfort?

5. What did you end up doing?

After answering these questions, see if you can repeat this exercise with other anger-provoking situations. The purpose is to identify which hot button is being pushed when your teen acts in a certain way. Is there a theme for that hot button?

You get upset because there is something unique to you and to no one else. Having an archeologist frame of mind for this task will take you a long way in learning from your anger and preparing you for the next skill: moving from working against your anger to working with your anger.

Let Anger Be

Angry behaviors are learned responses that may have become a habit for you when dealing with your teen struggling with high reactivity. Angry behaviors don't give you room to notice that you're not in control of your teen's behavior at all: your teen can think, behave, feel, and do as she chooses to, and getting upset with her won't change that. The only thing you're in control of is your own behavior, but getting fused with angry thoughts doesn't give you the room to step back from a situation, pause, and choose your parenting response. Siddhartha Guatama is attributed with saying, "Holding on to anger is like grasping a hot coal with the intent of throwing it at someone else; you are the one who gets burned."

Pure acceptance is the antidote to throwing the hot coals of anger at your teen. Acceptance is not giving your teen license to do whatever she wants, dismissing inappropriate behaviors, or liking and smiling in all situations. Acceptance is about cultivating an observer-like stance toward your experience from where you can pause and choose your behavior; acceptance is letting anger be without getting controlled by it.

Here are the five As to practice acceptance when feeling angry:

Accept the situation as it is.

Accept that you don't have to like the situation.

Accept your teen's behavior as it is.

Accept that you are feeling angry.

Accept that you are response-able to your anger.

For instance, Anna took acceptance to heart and reflected about a recent argument with her daughter Alissa. This is what she came up with:

Accept the situation as it is. *It's not ideal, but it's Sunday night, and I really would like to be relaxing in front of the TV, watching my favorite shows, but I'm here in the midst of a conflict with Alissa. I get it.*

Accept that you don't have to like this situation. *This is definitely far from ideal. I'm actually feeling trapped in this argument with Alissa. That's how it goes.*

Accept your teen's behavior as it is. *She seems very upset about not being able to bring marijuana to her birthday party. I can totally see how angry she is.*

Accept you are feeling angry. *It irritates me to no end that she just doesn't get it. How in the world am I going to tolerate my teen bringing her friends over to smoke marijuana in my house. Who cares if it's her birthday?*

Accept that you are response-able to your anger. *I didn't start this conflict, I don't like it, it totally irritates me, and I feel like screaming right now...and I know at the end it's up to me to figure out how to handle it, so I don't end up in a screaming match with Alissa.*

Putting into practice the five As will really give you the space to step back from anger-triggering moments and choose your parenting behavior instead of quickly acting on your anger and hurting yourself and your teen.

Choosing

The moment you choose to be curious and acknowledge accountability and response-ability for your angry behaviors, you also begin to accept all the uncomfortable feelings, memories, thoughts, and sensations that come along with anger, like sadness, frustration, powerlessness, judgment, criticizing thoughts, or your heart beating fast, to name few. Making room for that body and mind noise is a golden and crucial step that will give you an opportunity to really choose how to handle a situation.

Within ACT, this is one of the most fundamental invitations for parents in the midst of an angry moment. Are you willing to accept all that internal experience you go through for what it is and still choose to do what's effective in the direction of your parenting values in that precise moment of anger?

Choosing your parenting behaviors when you're not feeling triggered is one thing, but choosing your parenting behaviors in the midst of your own and your teen's internal struggles takes courage, and no one can make that call except you. No one is going to put a gun to your head when making a choice about how to live; the choice is always yours, even when you're hurting.

Sometimes you may choose to tame your angry behaviors. Other times, for a variety of reasons, you may intentionally choose to be angry. I invite you to pick up your parenting journal in those circumstances and answer the following questions:

Does anger make you feel energized?

Does being angry with your teen help you to avoid facing a tricky situation, a tricky feeling, or a tricky thought in that moment?

Do you hold the belief that by holding on to anger you're doing the right thing and sending a message to your teen?

What's the price you're paying for holding on to your anger?

Check for yourself how anger affects your relationship with your teen and family members in the long term. What are the health costs of anger for you? Are there any emotional costs in the long run? What's the impact of anger on your day-to-day life?

There are valid reasons for you to hold on to anger, but is holding on to anger effective in the long term? Let's see if you can learn to catch anger before it's too late.

EXERCISE: Preparing to Catch Anger Before It Catches You

Taming anger is a challenging task for any parent, especially if your teen's emotional switch goes on and off more often than not. This exercise prepares you to catch anger before it catches you by learning to have it and be curious about it without acting on it. I invite you to read the directions first slowly, recording them in your cell phone or any other device, and then listen to and follow the directions. It will probably take you fifteen minutes to complete this exercise at a reasonable pace.

Find a comfortable sitting position that allows your body to be relaxed. Close your eyes and slowly direct your awareness to your breathing. Allow yourself to notice every breath you take as you breathe in and breathe out. With every inhalation and exhalation, give yourself a chance to be present in this moment to the best you can while focusing on your breathing.

Now I'm going to invite you to imagine a recent angry episode you experienced with your teen in which you're not satisfied or pleased with how you handled it. See if you can recall the details of this scene, make it as vivid as possible, and do your best to recall it and even relive it as if it were happening in this precise moment. See if you notice the different thoughts accompanying this image. Can you name them for what they are? See if you recognize any blaming thoughts or judgment thoughts about your teen, then name them for what they are by saying *Here is a blaming thought, a judgment thought.* Maybe you're noticing a rule or expectation that your teen broke. Acknowledge it for what it is by saying *Here is a rule* or *Here is an expectation*, and keep identifying and naming those thoughts for what they are. See if you can distinguish a criticizing-story thought about your teen as a whole person. Then, as you did with the other thoughts, name it for what it is by saying *Here is a story thought.* Keep naming those thoughts as they come up, one by one. If you find yourself distracted, kindly and with intention bring your awareness back to the thoughts that are showing up in your mind while still focusing on the angry situation you're working on.

For the next couple of moments, try to switch the focus of your attention from your thoughts to your physical sensations while continuing to hold in mind the image of the angry moment you went through with your teen. Notice the physical sensations that are showing up in this moment. See if you can slowly scan your body from top to bottom while noticing any area filled with tension. See if you can notice any other physical reaction your body is having, such as your heart beating fast, shortness of breath, feeling hot, and as you did with your thoughts, see if you can be a detective and label the physical sensations that are present.

Next, see if you can gently return once again to the image of this angry memory you're working on and slowly start naming the emotions that accompany the angry feeling in the same way an archeologist would look at objects dug from the ground. Slowly bring your awareness to those emotions that cause you discomfort and pain and that may have fueled your anger to start with. Then, as you did with your sensations and your thoughts, name those feelings, one by one, by saying their name silently to yourself. Give yourself a chance to allow those uncomfortable emotions to be there; let them have their space; allow them to be, while noticing any urges to fight them, get rid of them, or eliminate them. Breathe, and kindly go back to noticing and naming those painful emotions. Notice the emotion of anger. You can even imagine stepping back while watching these feelings come and go, and as you do this, notice any wishes to distract yourself from the emotion of anger or any other painful feeling. Remember to breathe.

Now, if you're willing to continue working on that particular angry moment you went through with your teen, see if you can recall your behavior. See if you can recall your responses in this moment of anger. Can you see yourself responding to your teen? Once again, with gentleness, see if you can recall that particular moment in which you took action, notice any judgment or self-blaming thoughts, and while labeling those judgments or thoughts, as you did with other thoughts, bring your awareness to those moments in which you responded to this anger-provoking situation. Then ask yourself if your behavior was in agreement with your parenting values. Was it? Or was it not? No one can answer this question except you. Did you get closer to your teen because of this behavior? Or not? Allow yourself to notice any reaction when answering this question. No one can answer the question for you.

Finally, please take a couple of breaths and slowly allow yourself to come back into the room.

Take a couple of moments to reflect on this exercise and jot down your reactions in your parenting journal.

Now, see if you can practice the same exercise with other anger-provoking situations; the invitation is for you to allow yourself to go slowly, part by part, and prepare yourself to catch anger before it catches you.

In this last exercise, you practiced a skill based on a past angry situation, but you may have the thought *But it's so different when I'm in the middle of a battle with my teen.* And that's pretty real; anger flares up quickly sometimes. So here is what to do for…

Catching Anger in the Moment

Catching anger in the moment may feel like a colossal task when you're in the middle of a heated conversation with your teen. I can honestly tell you that although it's hard, it's not impossible, and little by little, you will notice how your skills get better and better, not just for you but for your teen and the people around you; everyone will get the benefits of your efforts at taming anger.

Catching anger in the moment starts with a very important step: commitment to yourself. Below, you will find a set of steps to go over in the moment when dealing with anger:

1. Commit to yourself to make a values-based choice: What type of parent do I want to be right now?

2. Press your feet against the floor, as hard as you can. Imagine that you're standing barefoot in sand and squish your toes down deep into the sand.

3. Breathe intentionally as slowly as possible, especially when you're exhaling.

4. Practice acceptance in the moment: the situation is what it is, your teen behaves as she behaves, you feel what you feel, and you're the owner of your responses (no one else).

5. Choose your behavioral response. Do you need to say no to your teen, make a request, or are you solving a conflict?

Every moment of anger is a moment of choice. Give it your best!

Watch Out for Your Internal Reactions

Do you recall all the benefits and applications of mindfulness? Mindfulness is very handy in moments of conflict, because if you fully and intentionally pay attention to your internal reactions in your body, you will recognize different bodily cues of your own reactivity and whether the situation is manageable or not.

Here is your task: while talking to your teen, see if you can notice any microchanges in your body, such as an increase in body temperature, heart beating faster than usual, hands making fists, rapid speech, or excessive frowning in your forehead. While noticing, do your best to go back to your breathing, a very powerful tool you have to slow down your internal reactions; even taking big and deep breaths multiple times will help.

If at some point you notice that your physiological reactions are intensifying, and breathing doesn't help you to slow down physiologically, then request your teen to stop the conversation, because your body may be going into a flooded state. *Flooding* is a physiological state in which the stress hormones of your brain are increasing, and as a result, it's hard to manage your behavioral responses to the intense emotions you're experiencing.

According to John Gottman and Nan Silver (1999), if your heartbeat is higher than 100 beats per minute, then your ability to regulate your parental behavior is compromised and no good will come of it.

If you're going through a state of flooding, you can do the following:

1. Ask your teen directly for a break, and let her know that you will continue the conversation at another time; schedule a time to continue the conversation. For example, you could say, "Can we please talk about this later? I need to take a break, but I assure you, we'll talk about this later on XX." Leaving the situation without explaining the rationale of your behavior to your teen could be a trigger for all types of responses on your teen's side, including a dismissive one.

2. Give yourself at least twenty-five minutes to return to more manageable levels of physiological arousal.

3. During those twenty-five minutes, make sure you don't engage in any activity that can lead your mind to ruminate

about what you're going through in the moment. For instance, calling a friend or a partner to complain about your teen's behavior is simply going to make it worse for you in the moment because you are just rehearsing how to get hooked on angry thoughts.

4. Practice defusion with all those angry thoughts that your mind is generating. It's mind noise at the end.

5. See if you can check in with yourself to see what's really upsetting about the situation.

If for any reason you cannot leave the situation—because you are in the car with your teen, for example—then do your best to be still. Practicing stillness translates into saying nothing, doing nothing, and simply being in the moment as a witness of your own experience. Notice the intensity of the mind-talk, the feelings, the sensations, and, while pressing your feet hard against the floor, be still. Every time there is a strong urge to do anything, ground yourself against the floor as if you were the trunk of a tree. Ground yourself with intention, with kindness, as a personal choice.

When you practice the above steps over and over, not only with your teen but in any situation in which you're handling anger, you are practicing hands-on how to handle anger in the heat of the moment and staying away from doing or saying things you may regret later. The more you try out these new shoes, the better you will be able to walk in them. You can be the parent you want to be instead of the parent that anger pushes you to be.

Summary and Looking Ahead

Unhooking your mind from myths about anger while making room for account-ability and response-ability when getting upset with your teen will help you to create a fulfilling and long-lasting relationship with her. Every moment of struggle with anger is a moment of choice to move from furious to curious behaviors, from fighting against anger to working with it, to practice acceptance when anger shows up, and to catch anger before it catches you.

Taming anger is easier said than done, but by reading this chapter and practicing all the skills in it, you are already making a difference for you, your teen, and your family. The first step always starts with making a commitment to yourself and choosing who you want to be when getting angry instead of letting anger choose for you.

At times, parents are left with resentment and other painful feelings because of those sticky moments, all the hard work, and the emotional investment they go through in dealing with their dysregulated teen. Bitterness or resentment can make it hard for any parent to be at their best when dealing with their teen...and learning forgiveness is what's necessary.

CHAPTER 16

"I Don't Know How to Let It Go": Forgiveness Skills

Bruce came for a therapy session to talk about his fourteen-year-old son, Ian. As soon as the door of my office was closed, he said in an angry tone of voice, "I hate all this, I can't believe how ungrateful he is after all I've done for him. I have put my life aside for him; it makes me sick to my stomach to realize that I have actually raised a person like this." He went on, "When I saw his suicidal note on Facebook, I was so angry that I couldn't stop thinking about it. What's wrong with him? He posted on Facebook that he was going to kill himself on his birthday, and guess what, I received all types of e-mails and phone calls from his friends, their parents, and my friends. I don't know if I'll ever forgive him for putting us through all this awkwardness. It's unbearable at times, and even his younger siblings are affected by all this: they know they cannot leave him alone."

Parent and teen relationships are complex, and they inevitably bring moments of frustration, struggle, and disconnection. Holding on to anger, guilt, or resentment will often lead you and your teen to more anger, sadness, and hours of rumination in which both of you are replaying the angry memory in an endless loop, either within your minds or with someone else. Do you want to get out of that vicious cycle of conflict with your teen and its related cousin, anger? If you do, then this chapter is for you. Having an adolescent struggling with emotion dysregulation problems is an invitation for you not only to learn a specialized set of parenting skills but also to truly love and forgive, as any relationship we care for invites us to do.

What Are Forgiveness Skills?

In ACT, learning forgiveness skills in some ways is learning to live by your values; even though you may have not chosen forgiveness as your individual value, there are parenting values that are universal for any parent, and forgiveness is one of them. Can you imagine that being the parent you want to be, you would hold on to resentment or anger toward your teen? Quite likely not.

What is forgiveness? It's a personal decision you make for yourself to pause from holding anger and grudges, and it's a behavior you can show toward yourself or your teen.

There are two important points that need to be highlighted: first, forgiving is a personal choice that no one can make for you; you make it for yourself and not for someone else. Second, forgiveness, as a behavior, is a skill that you can learn, and like any other skill, it will require practice.

Sometimes parents are fused with misconceptions about forgiveness. So, let's clarify that

1. Forgiving is not about dismissing the fact that your teen has hurt you by saying or doing upsetting things, such as making threats or screaming at you.

2. Forgiving is not about forcing yourself to reconnect with your teen after the door was slammed in your face.

3. Forgiving is not telling yourself it's okay that you called your teen names because you were angry with him.

Forgiveness, in a nutshell, is letting go of the past for your own well-being and as a personal choice. You have done your very best up to this point, but if you're like many parents who find themselves with innumerable challenges raising a teen struggling with emotional reactivity, it's quite likely that those ongoing cycles of conflict between the two of you have led you to hold on to resentment toward either yourself or your teen. Chapter 14 on conflict management and chapter 15 on anger showed you how you can make a shift in those rocky moments; the next pages will show you how to continue making that 180-degree turn away from reactive parenting toward values-based parenting.

Are You Ready to Forgive?

Are you willing to learn forgiveness skills? Pause, look within, and check your response. It's okay if you are not ready to forgive either yourself or your teen. This book is about helping you to be the parent you want to be, but no one can force that process on you. If you're not ready, go to the section entitled "If You're Not Ready to Forgive…" at the end of this chapter.

EXERCISE: Painful Memories Inventory

Pick up your parenting journal and take a couple of minutes to make an inventory of those memories of moments in which your teen has said or done something that still hurts or makes you angry despite your best efforts to let those memories go. Don't worry if what comes to mind is something that happened months or even years ago; the most important thing for this exercise is to write down all the memories you haven't been able to put behind you. Next to each memory in your inventory, write down all the emotions that come along with it.

For instance, when Bruce wrote his inventory about his painful memories of his son Ian, his inventory looked like this:

Painful memories about my teen that I cannot let go	Emotions
Receiving a call from the school because Ian was found smoking marijuana in the bathroom	Shame, anger, frustration, sadness
Finding Ian's cutting kit in his bathroom	Fear, sadness
Discovering a suicidal note in Ian's backpack along with a bottle of pills	Fear, exhaustion, anger, sadness
Reading Ian's post on Facebook about how awful his parent treats him and his denying that he receives any respectful treatment by me	Disappointment, embarrassment, sadness, confusion

After you have completed your inventory of hurtful or angry memories that are difficult to let go, it's time to switch directions. For this second part, write down a list of those memories you regret about things you have said or done to your teen and the emotions that come with it. Make this list even though you may have had the thought at the time that *I'm the parent, and I am entitled to discipline my teen.* This second part of the exercise may be difficult because it's hard to acknowledge that, despite your efforts, you may have made parental mistakes, sometimes intentionally, sometimes unintentionally.

When Bruce completed the second part of this exercise, his responses looked like this:

Painful memories about things I regret	Emotions
Dropping Ian at school and ignoring his request when he said, "Please don't drop me off at that corner. Some of the kids that tease me are standing there." In that moment, I simply told him, "Man up."	Shame, sadness
Screaming at Ian, "I can't take it anymore; I never knew that having a teen was going to be so difficult. If you think you don't need us, the door is open. You can march out and go any place you want."	Irritability, sadness
Telling Ian, "I don't care if your music equipment doesn't work. I only care that at least after 8:00 p.m. no one makes noise in the house, so we can rest."	Frustration, sadness

What were your reactions after completing this exercise? Were your reactions in the first and second parts similar or different? Feel free to jot down any reactions you may have had in your parenting journal.

Now, moving forward after identifying these painful memories, the next step is forgiveness in action.

EXERCISE: Forgiveness in Action

To start incorporating forgiveness in your parenting behaviors, do your best to complete this visualization exercise. First, read the instructions aloud and slowly, recording them in your cell phone or other device, and then play them back to yourself.

Choose a painful memory to focus on, either about forgiving yourself or forgiving your teen. It's better to pick a memory that is only mildly charged, since you're just beginning to practice forgiving skills.

After selecting the memory you wish to work on, ground yourself: press your feet really hard against the floor like the trunk of tree.

Take slow and deep breaths. Do your best to fill your belly with air, and then completely release the air through your nostrils.

Bring into your mind the memory you are working on as clearly as possible. See if you can visualize all the details of that painful memory, such as the colors, the sounds, the location, and the time of the day. Try to even hear the words that were said during that particular painful scene.

While holding this painful memory in mind, shift the focus of your attention to your body and see if you can notice any sensation or physical reaction you may be having at this moment.

Slowly and with intention see if you can name the feeling that is coming along with this painful memory. Can you make room for it? Can you notice the uniqueness of this emotion? Describe this feeling to yourself for what it is, a feeling, notice how it feels in your body, whether it's moving or not. If there are any judgments about this exercise, such as good or bad, kindly name them as judgments. If anger or resentment shows up, see if you can notice how anger or resentment feels in your body. What type of sensation shows up with anger or resentment? What's the quality of these sensations? Notice if there is any wish to push the anger, resentment, or any other emotion away.

Is your pain coming from the event itself or from holding on to the memory of the event? Is it possible that the memory of the event is the trigger to your pain? See if you can notice the pain that comes from holding on to this memory, dwelling on it, and replaying it over and over. The harder you hold on to it, the more waves of pain you go through.

See if you can become an emotion detective and explore other feelings or sensations that are showing up in this exercise as they come and go. Are you willing to notice how your emotions shift while you continue to work on this painful memory? Is the same emotion present? Is it a different one? Is the emotion as intense as the first one you recalled, or does it have a different intensity now? Can you simply notice the shift from one emotion into another from the beginning of the exercise to this point? Can you notice the shift in physical sensations from the beginning of the exercise to now?

See if you can offer yourself forgiveness by saying a forgiving phrase for what you have done, intentionally or unintentionally, wittingly or unwittingly.

Slowly bring your attention back to your breathing and stay with it for a while. Let your emotions settle into the spaciousness of your breath and awareness.

After finishing this exercise, jot down in your parenting journal any reflections you have; take your time to reflect on the experience. Finally, see if you can answer the following questions:

What's the payoff for forgiving my teen or myself in this moment? And is there something for me to learn from letting go of my resentment toward my teen or myself?

See if you can repeat this exercise at you own pace with each one of the memories you wrote down in the painful memories inventory. Forgiveness requires patience because it's an invitation to face the raw pain you have been carrying around. Are you ready to let go of your anger, resentment, and grudges toward your teen or yourself?

If You're Not Ready to Forgive...

No one said that forgiveness is an easy decision; in fact, it's one of the most difficult ones in any relationship. If you're not ready or you don't want to forgive for any reason, it's understandable. No one can force you to forgive—it's a personal choice—and certainly this book is not about that. The following questions and recommendations will help you to work through your ambivalence or stuckness with anger and resentment.

Is your mind ruminating or dwelling on the past? Is your mind bringing up to you all types of images and thoughts about those past painful memories? If your answer is yes, please go back and read chapter 15 on anger; you will benefit from completing those exercises again.

Are you experiencing a strong emotional reaction when bringing to mind those painful memories? Is it to the point that those feelings take over the moment? If that's the case, reread chapter 7 and go over the exercise called "Your Feelings" to practice how to handle an intense emotion.

After completing the exercises in this chapter, did you experience a strong sensation or sensations in your body to the point that your reactivity meter got elevated really quickly? If so, return to chapter 15 and revisit the exercise "Preparing to Catch Anger Before It Catches You." Physiology could easily betray you when your body reaches a place of high activation and you become a prisoner of your hormones and neurochemical reactions.

If you do not feel trapped by past thoughts or images or are not going through a chain of emotions or physical sensations, and you're still struggling with forgiveness, then answer the following questions in your parenting journal:

What's the payoff of holding on to anger and resentment toward your teen or yourself?

What is holding on to that upsetting memory really doing for you?

What would happen if you were able to forgive your teen or yourself in this precise moment?

Does being resentful and angry change what happened in the past?

What happens to the relationship with your teen if you continue to hold on to this resentment?

Answering the above questions will give you an insight into whatever is blocking you from forgiving. Forgiveness is a personal choice you make for yourself and no one else, when you're willing and ready to do so.

Summary and Looking Ahead

Holding on to resentment, anger, or shame is one of the most natural reactions when you have been hurt or when you have hurt another person. But, what's the payoff of holding on to those emotions? More anger, resentment, hours of dwelling, replaying over and over a past event in your mind, and at the end, more struggle. People will disappoint you, and you will disappoint them as well; that's the nature of all relationships. All relationships come with the sweet and the sour together, both sides of the coin. Parenting a teen suffering with high emotionality is learning to love and forgive him and yourself. Practicing forgiving your teen and yourself paves the way for both of you to begin to respond to painful experiences as a personal choice instead of allowing the pain to choose those responses for you or your teen. No one can make this decision for you or force you to forgive. In the end, this is another personal choice you make for yourself and not for someone else.

Here are suggestions for you to continue to practice forgiving behaviors: write a forgiving letter for yourself. Write a forgiving letter for your teen.

If, in this moment, your mind comes up with other thoughts, such as *I made mistakes, but that's nothing compared to what my teen has done to me and the family* or *Parenting is about disciplining, and I shouldn't be questioned by him*, then I invite you to name those thoughts for what they are (comparison thoughts, angry thoughts, to name a few) and check what their purpose is in this precise moment. What are those thoughts pushing you to do right now? Will acting on those thoughts take you toward or away from the parent you want to be? After answering those questions in your parenting journal, make a choice.

CHAPTER 17

"Why Do I Need to Be Kind?": Compassion Skills

How often do you experience moments of connection with your teen? When asked this question, parents of teens struggling with emotional sensitivity pause, ponder a bit, and sometimes recall sweet memories; other times they don't, as if feeling that connecting with their teen were almost a nonexistent experience. The large number of emotional crises that parents and teens go through together usually becomes part of a family's daily life, which makes it naturally harder for you or any parent to look at your teen as a person who is struggling and using all the skills she has in those moments; even though those skills are not helpful, that's all that she knows.

As some of the parents I work with describe, it's almost as if parenting has become a chore; even just the image of spending ten minutes in the car with your teen makes you feel stressed out, and your mind goes into disaster forecaster mode, anticipating an argument between the two of you. That's the time when you may notice that the master author of your mind starts speaking loudly, and naturally it's hard to be present in the moment and be receptive to other experiences.

All these challenges understandably lead you and any parent to go into a problem-solving mode to search for a solution to this problem, your "teen problem." Your mind needs to make sense of what's happening; and as a result, you find yourself spending hours and hours going over multiple reasons for your teen problem, such as your genetics, your partner's genetics, your partner's behaviors, or your teen's friends…the list of potential causes goes on and on. Your mind will relentlessly continue to look for a solution, because you're in pain, and your mind is simply doing its job, attempting to alleviate your pain.

I have seen two mind-solutions parents arrive at when searching for solutions to their teen problem: they either get fused with a blaming story about their teen or get hooked on a self-blaming story about themselves for what their teen and families are going through. What's the payoff of holding on to those blaming narratives about yourself or your teen? More hopelessness, disconnection, and sadness for you and your teen. This chapter is about making a shift from looking at yourself or your teen with harsh eyes and as a problem that needs to be solved to looking at yourself and your teen with compassionate eyes while accepting that both of you are struggling right now—not just you, not just your teen, but both of you.

What Is Compassion?

The etymology of the word "compassion" can be found in two Latin terms: *com-*, which means "together," and *pati*, which means "to bear or suffer." Therefore, compassion can be understood as "suffering or struggling together." Many spiritual traditions, such as Judaism, Christianity, Muslim, and Buddhism, have long emphasized compassion and its benefits.

Paul Gilbert (2010), a clinician and researcher from the University of Derby in the United Kingdom, drew on attachment theory, neuroscience, evolutionary theory, and Buddhist principles to develop a specific therapy model called compassion-focused therapy. For Gilbert, compassion includes both sensitivity to suffering and also a deep commitment to preventing and relieving that suffering in yourself and others. Gilbert identified three different affective systems in our brains that are important to understanding compassion: the incentive system, which is in charge of behaviors connected with wanting and pursuing; the affiliation system, which gives us a sense of safety and connection; and finally, the threat system, which regulates our need for safety. All these systems get activated and interact constantly through different daily life experiences, allowing us to go back and forth between our internal and our external worlds.

Here is the sensitive aspect of the interaction among these systems in parenting your teen: it's possible that frequent arguments and crises with her have led you to experience a degree of discomfort about your teen that activates your threat system, blocking any soothing or caring behavior for her. Therefore, because you're in threat mode, it's really hard to engage in any soothing or kind behavior for you or your teen.

Within ACT, as Tirch, Schoendorff, and Silberstein (2014) pinpointed, compassion-focused practices are already built throughout all of the skills you have been learning, and compassion is also a skill that can be learned, developed, and practiced intentionally. In this chapter, compassion is presented as a two-fold skill: compassion for yourself and compassion for your teen.

Why Is Compassion Important for You as a Parent?

Compassion is important when dealing with your teen because the more you get fused with the blaming story about yourself or your teen, the more disconnected and hopeless you may feel about raising her.

EXERCISE: Looking at Blaming Stories

Let's take a look at the impact of getting hooked on a blaming story about yourself as a parent. Pick up your parenting journal, bring into your mind a particular moment in which you were blaming yourself, and answer the following questions:

1. What was going on before the self-blaming story showed up in your mind?

2. What were the self-blaming thoughts or narratives your mind came up with?

3. What happened after you got hooked on the self-blaming thoughts or narratives? See if you can describe actions you took.

And finally, answer this last important ACT question: Were those actions helpful to be the parent you want to be?

After Seth completed this exercise, he came up with the following responses to the first three questions:

What was going on before: "I asked my son not to waste his entire day playing video games, and it turned into an argument."

Self-blaming thoughts/story: "It's my fault, I shouldn't have screamed at him."

"I shouldn't have reacted the way I did."

"I always screw things up with my teen."

I have failed my teen, myself, and my family."

What happens after: "Feeling defeated, sad, disappointed."

When Seth asked himself if those actions helped him be the parent he wants to be, he realized that his self-blaming thoughts led him to feel defeated, sad, and disappointed about himself as parent.

Self-blaming stories blind you, and any parent, from acknowledging that you and your teen are both struggling; self-blame also opens the door to getting hooked on the judgment machine, past- or future-oriented thoughts, feelings of rejection, and disconnection at the end.

Compassion skills could prevent you from making things worse for yourself or your teen, as they increase your ability to defuse from unhelpful mind-talk, acknowledge your pain and your teen's pain, respond to it kindly, and discover flexible ways to support yourself or your teen. Compassion skills won't solve all the painful issues you have with your teen, but they will certainly help you cope much better with the stress, so you can focus on getting unstuck and move toward being the parent you want to be.

It Feels Like You're Alone, But You're Not

Most parents I work with struggle with a sense of isolation because they may find it shameful to share with others what they are going through with their teens. Once, a father came into my office saddened after going to an event at his workplace and seeing his coworker and son hanging out together; his mind quickly went into comparison mode and slowly became filled with self-criticism: *You're the only one who messed up with your teen; no one else screwed this teen up, just you.* Other times, parents have a sense of shame about what they go through with their teens and do not know how they could possibly speak about it with other parents; a mother once said, "How can I tell my friend that my teen has been cutting and calling me names, when she's telling me her kids are going to apply for college, getting a job during the summer, and she can't believe how quickly they're moving on in life? How could I possibly tell her that I feel like hiding myself and wish I could make myself small?"

EXERCISE: You Are Not Alone

For the next exercise, slowly read the following directions, recording them in your cell phone or any other device, and then listen to them. This exercise may take approximately fifteen minutes.

Sit in a relaxed position, or if it's better for you, lean your body against a wall, but do your best to find a comfortable position. For the next couple of moments, see if you can start focusing on your breathing, notice every time you inhale and exhale, notice the passing sensations of the air while you breathe in and breathe out. Notice the rhythm and pace of your breathing, the sensation of air as it enters your nostrils and moves through your body; you can even notice the temperature of the air as it moves and leaves your body a few moments later.

If your mind brings distracting thoughts in this moment, it's natural; you're invited to notice these distracting thoughts as they come, and without reacting to them, name them for what they are, *distracting thoughts*, or choose any other name that resonates with

179

you. Let these distracting thoughts drift by like clouds in the sky, and gently go back to focusing on the flow of your breath.

Imagine for the next couple of moments one of those situations in which you felt you made a mistake with your teen. See if you can bring that image into your mind as clearly as possible and for a couple of moments hold on to that image. Silently describe the feeling or feelings that show up for you. See if you can locate any sensations in your body and notice whether that sensation stays in the same location or it moves through your body. See if you can notice this sensation without pushing it away or trying to get rid of it, just letting it be. Notice the stream of thoughts, if any. See if you can notice how difficult that moment was, how difficult it was to be in your shoes in that situation. You were doing the best you could in that moment, and you are aware that you are not perfect as a parent, as no parent is. See if you can notice your reactions in this moment while acknowledging that all parents have made mistakes while doing their best in the moment.

See if you can make room in this moment to accept that all parents share being imperfect. You are not alone. You are part of a community of parents out there who struggle as you do. Parenting a teen struggling with emotional vulnerability is hard for you and for all parents. You are not alone. See if you can tell yourself with a soft and caring tone of voice that your pain as a parent of a teen with emotion dysregulation problems is the same pain that other parents feel. You are in the same boat with other parents, sharing the pain and imperfections of being a parent of a teen with emotional-sensitivity problems. See if you can make room to accept this experience, your experience and the experience of others, accepting it for what it is.

Notice how it feels in your body to accept your imperfection and other parents' imperfections. Notice any reaction in your body in this moment of acceptance without blaming. Notice if there is even a tiny sensation taking form in your body, and see if you can name the feeling that comes with that sensation. See again if you can tell yourself, in a kind and soothing voice, that it's not easy to be in your shoes. It's not easy to be a parent. It's not easy to feel alone, and yet, you're not alone. Slowly go back to paying attention to the flow of your breath while breathing in and breathing out. Allow yourself to take a couple of slow and deep breaths before finishing this exercise.

After finishing this compassion exercise, grab your parenting journal, and jot down any reactions you had to it.

Holding on to self-blaming thoughts about your parenting role makes you want to hide your struggle, because you feel like you're all alone, but your experience parenting an emotionally sensitive teen is more common than you could imagine in these moments.

Self-Compassion in Practice

Self-compassion is the skill of acknowledging your own distress and responding to yourself with the same consideration and kindness that you would show to someone you care for who was in similar distress.

EXERCISE: Practicing Self-Compassion

Let's move on to practicing self-compassion for the next couple of moments. Make sure you find a quiet space, budget fifteen to twenty minutes, and have your parenting journal next to you. Then, slowly and intentionally read these guidelines.

1. Ground yourself by focusing on your breathing, noticing the qualities every time you're inhaling and exhaling.

2. Write down all those self-blaming thoughts you hold about your parenting role.

3. Read them slowly and aloud to yourself for a moment.

4. Notice any reaction you have and how it feels to get caught by those self-blaming thoughts.

5. Can you make space for your reactions to these self-blaming thoughts for what they are? No need to push them away, run away from them, or distract from them. Can you let those reactions be?

6. Notice how it feels to just have those reactions to the self-blaming thoughts without acting on them, simply having them.

7. See if you can give a name to this self-blaming parenting voice your mind comes up with.

8. Now, imagine your best friend is next to you, has listened to your self-blaming voice, and is responding to you. What would your friend say? Write down these responses in your parenting journal.

9. Read aloud those responses and notice your reactions to them. How did it feel? What thoughts came to you? Any sensations?

10. Before moving forward, see if you can focus on your breathing again and for a couple of moments gently pay attention to every time you're breathing in and breathing out.

11. Go back to step 2 at the beginning of this exercise where you wrote down those self-blaming thoughts, and read them aloud to yourself.

12. Notice again your reactions to this self-blaming voice by paying gentle attention to those feelings, thoughts, sensations, and even urges that may have shown up to you.

13. Now imagine that a very compassionate voice within you has listened to your self-blaming thoughts and is responding to you. This compassionate voice is caring, kind, and holds those self-blaming thoughts lightly, for what they are: just thoughts and words, not as facts. This compassionate voice notices your struggle when hearing those words and sees your suffering. This compassionate voice knows how it feels to be in your shoes when having those self-blaming thoughts and sees your pain.

14. See if you can make room for this compassionate voice and imagine what it will tell you right now; see if you can make room for this compassionate voice by softening your tone of voice, relaxing your facial muscles, and really talking to yourself from a place of caring. Write down these compassionate responses.

15. Slowly read aloud those compassionate responses.

16. And now see if you can scan any reactions to listening to those compassionate responses. As you have been doing previously, see if you can notice any emotions, sensations, thoughts, or urges showing up in this moment for you.

17. Finish this exercise by gently going back to paying attention to your breathing and slowly noticing the subtleties of breathing in and breathing out.

Finally, answer for yourself this last question: what type of relationship do you really want to have with yourself as a parent when those self-blaming thoughts pop up in your mind?

This exercise is the beginning of incorporating self-compassion into your parenting life; it may feel awkward at the beginning, but the more you learn to get unhooked from those self-blaming thoughts, the more space you're going to have to be the parent you want to be and to choose your parenting behaviors from that place.

Practicing Self-Compassion in Your Daily Life

It's quite unlikely that while living your daily life and doing all the errands you have to do, you will always find time to be in a quiet place for fifteen minutes. Most of the parents I work with don't have that time. In fact, they usually say that finding fifteen minutes or even one minute for themselves is a luxury in their day. So, part of our work together is to find ways to practice self-compassion in a way that allows you to continue moving through your day. Here is what I usually recommend parents do for practicing self-compassion in their daily life when those self-blaming thoughts get loud and prevent them from making choices.

1. Ground yourself with your breathing (this is highly recommended).

2. Accept the emotion that comes with the self-blaming thoughts.

3. Notice the quality of these self-blaming thoughts.

4. Name the self-blaming thoughts. (For instance, Seth decided to name his self-blaming story as "amygdala talk" because, in his experience, those self-blaming thoughts came along with large waves of hopelessness, guilt, and frustration, as if the emotions had a life or their own and demanded attention, just as the amygdala demands attention when activated.)

5. Let those self-blaming thoughts go. (You can imagine placing each self-blaming thought in a balloon and seeing the balloon fly up in the air. Or you can count the times when the self-critical voice comes up; you can even keep track of those times in your cell phone or in a little paper in your wallet by using checkmarks each time the thought comes. Any other ideas for letting those self-blaming thoughts go?)

6. Commit to your choice.

If it's hard for you to get unhooked from those self-blaming thoughts because they seem so real, it's okay. You're still making a choice, and it's certainly not easy to shift gears when handling these self-blaming thoughts. It's hard and yet not impossible to do. It certainly took a lot of commitment on my part to learn these skills and let those self-blaming thoughts go, but as we say within the ACT community, our personal commitment is not to a perfect outcome but to the process: the process of living our values by starting again even if we don't succeed the first time.

Incorporating self-compassion into your parenting life may feel awkward at the beginning, as it does with any new practice; however, it also offers you another choice to make when those self-blaming stories come up for you.

From Self-Compassion to Compassion for Your Teen

At the root of your emotional needs, your teen's emotional needs, and every human being's emotional needs, there is the same need for affection, caring, acceptance, forgiveness, and love. So, instead of focusing on the differences of opinion or disagreements about how to live life and to be in the world, between you and your teen, compassion skills are about recognizing the commonalities of your struggle and your teen's struggle. You both are hurting, not just you, not just her.

EXERCISE: Practicing Compassion for Your Teen

Here is a brief exercise to practice compassion skills toward your teen. Make sure to have your parenting journal at hand and budget approximately ten minutes to complete this exercise.

1. Bring in your mind, as a clearly as possible, a specific argument you and your teen had recently.

2. While holding on to this memory, do your best to slow down and notice your reactions to this argument by paying attention to the thoughts, emotions, sensations, and even urges you had in that moment, based on this memory.

3. Write down your reactions, read them to yourself, and pause for a moment.

4. Now, on another page, and holding still to the same memory, see if you can imagine your teen's point of view and for a moment try to notice the thoughts, emotions, sensations, and even urges she may have had as if you were in her shoes.

185

5. As you did before, write down your responses, read them to yourself, and pause again.

6. Using another page, draw a line down the middle of it. And looking at what you wrote about this argument based on your point of view and imagining your teen's point of view, see if you can notice any similarities between your struggles and your teen's struggles, and write them down in the left column. Then see if you can notice any differences between your pain and your teen's pain about this situation, and write them down in the right column.

7. See if you can make your compassionate voice present in this moment and imagine how your compassionate voice will respond to your teen's pain. What would this compassionate voice tell your teen? Write down your responses.

8. Now, imagine how your compassionate voice will respond to your pain in that moment. What would this compassionate voice tell you right now? Write down your responses.

Moving forward with practicing compassion skills, see if you can practice this exercise not only when recalling an argument you had with your teen but also when recalling when your teen was struggling with a particular issue totally unrelated to the relationship with you, such as rejection from a person she likes romantically, disappointment because someone didn't text her back, sadness because she feels that she doesn't fit within her group, and so on. If you recall from chapter 11, to practice empathy skills, you ask, accept, acknowledge verbally your teen's experience, and ask directly what you can do to help your teen in that moment. When adding compassion skills, the question for you is, what would the compassionate voice within you tell her about her pain and that moment of struggle?

Compassion is a vital skill for handling harsh thoughts, seeing your own and your teen's struggles with caring eyes, and creating sweet moments of connection between the two of you. Life is a rollercoaster of experiences and full of moments of joy, happiness, and excitement as well as sadness, struggle, pain, and hurt. No one better than you can teach your teen how to hold all those experiences and still make the best of every moment you have in your hands with a touch of caring.

Summary and Looking Ahead

The reality of raising a highly sensitive teen is far from what you may have imagined when becoming a parent. The reality of dealing with a teen suffering with emotion dysregulation problems is that you are going to make mistakes, as your teen will make mistakes. Sometimes you are going to be very angry or your teen is going to be very angry; sometimes, despite your efforts, it will be challenging to forgive yourself or your teen; and sometimes things will go wrong, terribly wrong. What does your mind do in those moments? Your mind will do its job and it will try to find a cause of your pain. Your mind will also lecture you to do a better job or will hold stories about yourself or your teen not trying hard enough. The self-blaming talk or blaming talk toward your teen may motivate you sometimes, but when it becomes habitual, the outcomes are usually different: the more you get hooked on those self-blaming thoughts or blaming stories about your teen, the more stuckness, resentment, and hopelessness you're going to feel.

Here are three other exercises to continue incorporating compassion practices into your parenting:

Grab your parenting journal and write down how you imagine your compassionate self. Allow yourself to write down what type of facial expressions you would have, what your body posture would look like, how you would talk, speak, what tone of voice you would use, and even the rhythm and speed of your voice.

As another exercise, think and write about a situation that provoked anger or irritation when dealing with your teen. Describe the triggers, your behavior, and the outcomes for yourself. Then on another sheet of paper, draw a line down the middle of the page. On the left side, write down the reactions from your angry self to this situation, and on the right side, write down the reactions from your compassionate self to this situation. At the end, notice both responses and write down anything you learned from contrasting these two very different responses.

Looking at the same situation that provoked anger or irritation when dealing with your teen, respond to it from three different viewpoints: your housewife or stay-at-home dad self, your struggling self, and your compassionate self. Afterwards, answer these questions: what would your struggling self tell your housewife or stay-at-home dad self if listening to those self-attacking thoughts? And what would your compassionate self tell your struggling self and your housewife or stay-home-dad self if listening to those self-attacking thoughts?

PART 4

When Things Get Rocky

CHAPTER 18

"Let's Drop the Feminine Crap!": For Fathers and Male Caregivers*

"Why should I be like my wife? This whole thing of appreciating is just not my thing. When do I talk like that to anyone? Not even my wife...and why should I talk to my teen like this? I just want results. I just want a good outcome. I cannot pretend to be who I'm not. I'm not a softy, like my wife or my daughter. I'm just myself, and this is just how I talk and how I'm in the world." Some of the fathers or male caregivers of the teens I work with have made comments like these. Their mind is simply doing its job, like a popcorn machine, coming up with all the different thoughts they have been exposed to growing up as males.

If you're the father or male caregiver of a boy (and we're making a generalization), then you probably relate to one of the biggest goals: preparing your teen to become a man. Traditionally, this preparation involves messages like "stop acting like a girl" if he sheds tears, expresses joy, or shows fear. As long as your son isn't behaving in ways that mirror traditional feminine behavior, then he's earning his man cards. However, if you have a daughter, it's likely she doesn't shoulder the same yoke; no one demands of her "to woman up" or "be a real woman." But if she shows emotionality, your mind may come up with categorizing thoughts like *This is what girls do* and even judgment thoughts: *Girls are weak; they're emotional.* Showing emotional vulnerability and asking for help are behaviors perceived

* (Chapter written in collaboration with Andrew Reiner, MFA, Lecturer, Towson University Honors College)

as signs of weakness for both men and women but particularly for men; men are taught to mask, hide, and bottle up their feelings as much as possible unless it's anger, even if angry behaviors destroy their relationships and alienate the people they love. Your mind has also been trained to come up with reasons about the benefits of teaching boys and girls to be emotionally strong; after all, you don't want them to be bullied or taken for a wimp or a pushover as they get older. Yet, placing these rigid expectations on your teen is actually backfiring.

The Dark Side of Asking Teens to "Man Up"

Research has consistently indicated that suppressing, masking, or avoiding uncomfortable emotions can, in fact, further entrench them and make them stronger and more powerful; the more you avoid and push down these unwanted emotions, the more they fester (Hayes et al. 2004). For instance, if you were feeling sad because someone you cared about passed away and you wanted to avoid feeling down, you might drink a beer or distract yourself with TV, pretending as if nothing had happened, as parents do when using the pusher emotion management strategy, if you recall from chapter 7. However, you still feel down, and as soon as the alcohol tapers off from your body or you're not keeping yourself busy with TV, it will simply emerge again. The more you try to avoid sadness, the worse you feel in the long term. Similarly, getting fused and acting on the thought of asking teens to "man up" is like asking them to deny, suppress, and dismiss their emotions.

Let's take a look at this problem with ACT lenses on.

Less Pliance, More Tracking

As you may recall, ACT is based on the relational frame theory (RFT) of language; this theory about language, at its core, suggests that our mind carries on all the derived relations among symbols, such as words, images, memories, and feelings, that are established throughout our life because of our learning history. There are two processes that RFT refers to quite often: *tracking* and *pliance*. These two processes are very handy for understanding how some beliefs are stronger than others regardless of how much we try to be independent thinkers.

Pliance occurs when we behave based on a derived relation of symbols without even noticing them; for example, if you grew up in a household in which the roles of man and woman were rigidly defined, you have been naturally exposed to what is "proper" social behavior for a man and a woman, such as the man is a provider, is stronger, is a protector, never cries, doesn't show emotions in general, and the woman is a caregiver—nurturing, soft, and emotional. Because of pliance, every time you see a woman, you quickly associate her with high emotionality without even knowing her.

Tracking, on the contrary, is about noticing those derived relations among words, images, memories, feelings, and so on, established throughout our learning history, and distinguishing them from our direct experience. For instance, following with the previous example, when looking at a woman expressing emotion, your mind may come up with thoughts such as *It's natural, all women are emotional*, but because of tracking, you notice that thought, have it as a hypothesis, and do your best to learn how this woman is when showing emotion, distinguishing whatever association you have about women from the person in front of you.

Now let's zoom in on all those messages you have received, either explicitly or not, when growing up and how they may or may not be showing up when parenting your teen.

When Growing Up...

We all have been socialized within different contexts, starting in our household, school, group of friends, and later on with coworkers. Within each social context, we have learned—through being explicitly told, by observation, or by direct experience—certain ways to behave associated with the constructs of being a man or a woman. Let's do a brief exercise to notice or *track* these associations your mind holds.

EXERCISE: Tracking Your Associations About Men and Women

Grab your parenting journal, go back in time to your childhood and adolescence, and complete these statements as they apply to you, filling in with as many associations as you can recall for each one:

"My mother said that women are good at..."

"My father said that women are good at..."

"My mother said that men are good at..."

"My father said that men are good at..."

"My mother said that women are bad at..."

"My father said that women are bad at..."

"My mother said that men are bad at ..."

"My father said that men are bad at..."

Now complete the next statements about how your parents handled different situations like conflict, sadness, and so on:

"When feeling stressed, my mom..."

"When feeling stressed, my dad..."

"My dad showed me affection by..."

"My mom showed me affection by..."

"When my mom was angry, she..."

"When my dad was angry, he..."

"When feeling sad or down, my dad..."

"When feeling sad or down, my mom..."

Take a couple of minutes to read your responses. There is no right or wrong response; you're simply noticing how your mind is coming up with all those derived associations about the words "men," "women," "dad," and "mom," and behaviors that come associated with them because of your upbringing. Let's take this a step further and see how other experiences you have had, in addition to the ones learned within your family, may have contributed to associations about your role as a man and a father. Grab your parenting journal and complete these statements:

"My mind says that a father is better than a mother at..."

"My mind says that a mother is better than a father at..."

"My mind says that when raising children, a mother is supposed to..."

"My mind says that when raising children, a father is supposed to..."

"My mind says that when dealing with emotions, a father should..."

"My mind says that when dealing with emotions, a mother should..."

Now, let's pay attention to what your mind comes up with when thinking about how your highly sensitive teen is misbehaving. Complete these statements:

"When my teen doesn't follow my directions, I..."

"When my teen starts crying, I..."

"When my teen screams back at me, I should..."

"If my teen accuses me of minimizing his or her problems. I usually..."

"If my teen feels down or sad, I tend to...

"Do I handle things differently if my teen is a boy or a girl?"

After completing your responses, see if there are any similarities or differences between how you were raised and how you are raising your teen and teaching your teen to handle emotions. Have you been fused with beliefs about masculinity when raising your teen? The response is yours.

Your mind will naturally come up with all types of thoughts, anytime, anywhere. It's possible that while reading a particular section in this book your mind came up with thoughts along the lines of *This is too feminine* or *I'm being asked to show a weak response.* I invite you to notice those thoughts, write them down, and write down the parenting behaviors associated with them. For instance, Ramsy came up with this: "When thinking about appreciation skills, my mind said, *This is just showing weakness to my teen, and no one talks like this in real life.* Then I usually don't compliment my teen and don't even notice what he may be doing right at home or school. When reading the assertiveness chapter, I noticed the thought, *This a bunch of soft talk to say 'no' to my teen,* and in general, I respond to his request by saying no in a very firm tone of voice, so he doesn't come back to me with more questions."

Noticing when you're getting fused with any of these historical thoughts about masculinity is the first step to answering a very important question in ACT: *How is it working?* When you get fused with those beliefs about being a man and act on them, what happens to the relationship with your teen? What are you really teaching your teen about emotionality?

At the end of the day, these are the questions you are invited to ask yourself: is this really the legacy you want to pass on? Do you really want your teen to become yet another faceless statistic in the spiking numbers of teens struggling with emotional dysregulation?

A Different Response…

Here is an alternative response for all those moments in which past or future thoughts, rules, or judgment thoughts along the lines of *Man up, Be strong, Stop acting like a girl,* or *Don't show your emotions* show up in your mind when dealing with your teen: defusion. Here is how to get unhooked from those thoughts:

1. Notice them.

2. Name them: you can also give these types of thoughts a name, such as "Here comes Mr. Muscle," "Mr. Big Man,"

"the weak story," "the feminine crap story," or any other name that allows you to recognize when those thoughts are showing up in your mind.

3. Imagine for a moment those thoughts are like uninvited neighbors showing up to your birthday party, and you have a choice to make. Do you get upset and let them know how angry you are, or do you notice them and do what's important to you in that moment, so you can continue enjoying your birthday party?

This defusion exercise will help you have those thoughts and choose your parenting response instead of quickly getting trapped by them.

Sometimes, without even realizing it, you may get caught by these stories. No problem. The moment you realize that has happened, just name it: *Oh boy, I just got hooked by "the feminine crap story."* It's natural. Learning to be flexible with your thoughts is a process, and throughout this book, you have been invited to commit to the process of parenting the best you can, and not to perfect parenting. Over time, defusing from these stories, letting them go, and behaving as the parent you want to be when dealing with your emotionally sensitive teen will get easier. The more you choose your parenting response, the better it gets.

CHAPTER 19

"Am I Willing?": Moments of Choice

Here we are: the final chapter. Before you close this book, let me share something with you: I discovered ACT in 2003, and my initial reactions were skepticism and frustration with an approach totally different from what I had learned as a therapist up to that point; it wasn't an easy journey, and it took me hundreds of hours of reading, talking to people, listening to podcasts, attending workshops—you name it—but in that process, I found what truly matters to me as a clinician, a person, a daughter, a partner, and as a friend. I discovered that "creating intimacy" is a fundamental value in my relationships and, in particular, the relationship with my mom. Every week when I talked to my mom, I made the point of asking her questions about her daily struggles when teaching, hopes for her students, worries about her health, concerns about her cooking, and so on. I also made the point to share with her my fears about not being a good enough daughter, trips I want to take, recent movies I watched, new music I listened to do, worries about my career, and so on. It wasn't easy, because every time I talked to my mom, my mind came up with hundreds of thoughts like: *She doesn't know who I am; she won't understand me; she won't get it*; and *Why does she need to be worried about the neighbor's cat?* Quite often I even had the urge to tell her "Everything is fine" and hang up the phone as quickly as possible.

Every values-based step we take comes with the inevitable sweetness and sourness of life, and I certainly made mistakes when moving toward creating intimacy in the relationship with my mom.

It wasn't easy, but the more I asked her questions and shared what was going on with me, the more it became very clear that my struggle was worth it.

Through living my personal values, I learned that there is no other way of living life. Once you savor a life with meaning, it just gets better, and then suddenly it not only becomes natural, but you also discover that there is no going back to other ways of living, because they are empty.

Parenting a teen struggling with emotion dysregulation has good and sweet moments, but it's also a path full of frustration, stress, and sadness, because it's full of emotional turmoil. Parenting your teen without having clarity about your values, it is as if you were just mechanically walking in a desert with no way to discern what direction to go.

You have learned all the different ACT skills to handle those moments when your teen's emotional switch goes on and off, too much, too quick, too soon, and you have natural urges to use old unworkable emotional strategies, such as the pusher, the disconnector, the externalizer, or the surrenderer, or you're getting fused with judgment thoughts, stories about yourself or your teen, rules, and past or future thoughts. Making a shift to be the best parent possibly you can be, take actions toward your parenting values, and improve the relationship with your teen for the long run is doable, but it requires an extra ingredient: willingness.

Willingness: A Secret Power

You may recall the importance of "willingness" from chapter 8, in which you identified your parenting values, specific actions to take in line with them, and potential blocks in your values path. Now that you are at the end of the book and have learned all the different ACT skills, it's important to revisit this essential question about willingness.

Even when you're committed to making a 180-degree turn in your parenting behavior, it's to be expected that the dictator, judgment machine, time machine, or master author of your mind, along with painful emotions, impulses, and even physical sensations, will try to take you off the course of parenting using new ACT skills. It's natural to be tempted, because your mind is simply doing its job: it's attempting to use old tools that you learned before and are familiar with when dealing with your teen.

But what happens when you acted quickly, attempted to neutralize, or pushed away uncomfortable emotions? To answer this question, remember a time when you felt a sense of powerlessness when dealing with your teen and you tried to push down this feeling by quickly getting upset or disconnecting from her and abruptly removing yourself from the situation. Even though physically disconnecting from your teen reduced your feeling of powerlessness and worked for a moment, it's really a matter of time before it shows up again and potentially with more intensity.

And what happens when you get hooked on those judgments, past or future thoughts, rules, or stories about yourself or your teen and quickly act on them in your parenting life? Can you recall the last time you saw your teen as selfish, unappreciative, or ungrateful, and you ended up yelling those names at her? Or what happened when you thought about yourself as a bad parent and ended up not showing up for the conversation with your teen because you were too busy paying attention to your mind-talk? Behaving quickly on those thoughts may seem to work in the short term, but in the long term, those thoughts don't help to improve the relationship with your teen, and they take you far away from being the parent you want to be.

Now, imagine for a moment that those tricky thoughts, emotions, memories, and sensations are like a ball in a pool. The deeper you try to push the ball under the water, the more powerfully the ball pops out. In a similar way, the deeper you try to push down or replace your feelings of powerlessness, thoughts about yourself or your daughter, the more they're going to pop out. But if you let the ball float on the surface of the water for a while, without trying to grab or push it under, it will likely drift to the other side of the pool; similarly, the more you're willing to have those judgment thoughts along with those distressful emotions without responding to them or pretending you like them, but instead simply noticing them, the more manageable it's going to be. For instance, to pursue her value of connection, Marilyn committed to drive her daughter every weekend to her girlfriend's home one and a half hours each way; she was willing to make room for her feelings of frustration, impatience, and thoughts like *This is a waste of my time; she will respond with monosyllabic responses as usual; she doesn't even appreciate my efforts,* because she really wanted to learn about her daughter. Her willingness enabled her to hear about some of her daughter's struggles at school and to even learn the lines of one of her daughter's favorite characters in an animated film.

Willingness is the only way to handle all those internal blocks that show up on a daily basis in your parenting life, whether those blocks are distressing feelings, physical sensations, thoughts, or impulses. Willingness is a personal choice you make to respond to those blocks every parenting moment you have with your teen. Every time there is an internal obstacle showing up under your skin, you can respond to it in one of two ways. One, you get hooked on it and do your best to get rid of, suppress, avoid, or quickly act on it; the challenge is that getting hooked on that internal obstacle, whatever form it has, is relying on old parenting behaviors that make things worse with your teen, hurt your relationship, and take you far away from the parent you really want to be.

The other way to respond to those internal obstacles is to notice them, even though you don't like them, and willingly choose your response as a personal choice, by saying no to getting caught by those blocks and saying yes to your parenting behavior. Saying yes to your values-based parenting behavior is saying yes to you as the parent you strive to be for your teen. Here is a treasure: acting on your parenting values doesn't guarantee a path free of conflict with your teen or that those challenging memories, images, feelings, and thoughts will go away. Parenting with willingness is about taking steps toward the parent you want to be while carrying those inner experiences and without even knowing the outcome. And you may be thinking right now, *If it's not about getting rid of my internal obstacle, what's the treasure?* The more you behave as the parent you want to be when relating to your teen, the more you will experience a sense of vitality, fulfillment, and resilience to handle those rocky moments. And the more you do it with openness, caring, and putting in practice all the ACT skills you've learned in this book, the better it's going to be for you, your teen, and your relationship.

Here is the key willingness question to ask yourself moving forward: when dealing with your teen and feeling triggered by what she's saying or doing, are you willing to have those thoughts, memories, sensations, feelings, and urges and still do what matters to you as a parent in that particular moment? Are you willing to have all that uncomfortable inner experience that emerges when dealing with your teen and still take steps toward the parent you want to be by using your ACT skills?

Once again, answering this question and practicing willingness is a personal choice you make. And while most parents I work with find that these ACT skills have been positive for them in so many ways, it's important to remember that they're not the Constitution of the United States of America. You will make your own choices when dealing with your teen. Checking your willingness meter and practicing willingness is something you are invited to do by choice.

Moments of Choice

The choice about how to behave when parenting your teen is yours, and it will always be yours. Every moment with your teen, not only a conflictive one, is a moment to ask and answer for yourself the willingness question.

Using your ACT skills when you're not upset is one thing, but using them when feeling triggered when dealing with your teen is a different story. As one of my clients said once, "Dealing with my teen at home is one thing, but dealing with my teen when we're at my in-laws, and I quickly see him making all those remarks while getting upset with his grandfather, is like using all my willpower to not explode in the moment."

Within ACT you're invited to choose from moment to moment; however, you cannot choose your parenting behavior unless you pause first. So let's pause in this moment. How do you pause? By grounding yourself first, stomping your feet on the ground as if you were the trunk of a tree, and then choosing your values and your parenting behavior. This idea of pausing is not an easy one at the beginning of a potentially difficult situation, but it certainly gets more natural the more you do it. Being in your own shoes is not easy, and being in your teen's shoes is not easy either. It's hard for both of you. Keep in mind that life will bring many moments of distress, anxiety, sadness, and conflict to your teen, and who better than you to teach her those life skills so she can be the best person possible?

So, let's start by practicing how to choose your parenting behaviors for a particular parenting value. If you have more than one parenting value, choose one you want to work with for the purposes of the exercise.

EXERCISE: Your Moments of Choice

This exercise is based on the choice point exercise developed by Ciarrochi, Bailey, and Harris (2014). Grab your parenting journal, recreate the chart below, and use it to describe a sticky situation with your teen, the internal barriers your face, your moment-of-choice question, and how you could choose to respond with old behaviors (or hooks) or new behaviors (or helpers) using your ACT skills.

Moments-of-Choice Worksheet	
Parenting value:	
Sticky situation:	
Internal barriers (thoughts, images, sensations, urges):	
Moment-of-choice question: Which path will take me toward the parent I want to be?	
Old behaviors or "hooks"	**New behaviors or "helpers"**
Consequences of the "hooks"	**Consequences of the "helpers"**

After completing this exercise, see which behaviors are more helpful to live your parenting values: your hooks or your helpers. For instance, when Suzanne completed this exercise, she came up with the following:

Moments-of-Choice Worksheet	
Parenting value: *Caring.*	
Sticky situation: *Tell Catherine to stop calling her sister names if she doesn't want to spend time with her.*	
Internal barriers (thoughts, images, sensations, urges): *Thoughts: As soon as I tell her, she's going to start screaming and denying that she calls her sister names; next thing I know, I'm going to be accused of "having a favorite daughter"; my whole day is going to be ruined. Emotions: fear, frustration, disappointment, guilt. Sensations: tightness in my chest. Urges: to not say anything to Catherine.*	
Moment-of-choice question: *Which path will take me toward the parent I want to be?*	
Old behaviors or "hooks"	**New behaviors or "helpers"**
Saying nothing to Catherine. *Demanding that Catherine "behave nicely" with her sister.* *Asking Catherine's Dad to talk to her.* *Sending notes to Catherine's teacher, so she can talk to her.* *Threatening Catherine with sending her to therapy for the whole year.*	*Naming my future-oriented thoughts as "Suzanne the fortune-teller."* *Breathing slowly when noticing the sensation of fear and recognizing my urges.* *Noticing my urges to disconnect from Catherine.*
Consequences of the "hooks"	**Consequences of the "helpers"**
Catherine will stop talking to me, will avoid me for a week, won't talk at dinnertime. I'll feel hurt and awful about the mom I am.	*I know I'll have done my best to be an assertive mom.*

You can make every moment a moment of choice in your parenting life. The choice is paying attention to what will move you toward or away from your parenting values, as Suzanne did when noticing her hooks and helpers when taking behavioral steps toward her parenting value of caring.

When Things Get Rocky

Perfection doesn't exist; perfect parenting behaviors don't exist either. You may have encountered a moment in which you were hanging out with your teen, and things seemed to be going well until your sweet teen suddenly told you how much she hates you because you don't want her to smoke weed. Then you found yourself silently noticing all the inner noise in your head, and you asked yourself the willingness question, but the next thing you did was scream back at your teen. Everything seemed to be going well in your outing with your teen, and you were committed to handle the situation as you have learned in this book, but then it happened: your old parenting behaviors came back.

As Kelly Wilson and Troy Dufrene (2010) pointed out, sometimes things might go wrong, terribly wrong. Let's go over one of those moments when things went wrong in your parenting job.

EXERCISE: When Things Went Wrong

Grab your parenting journal and write down a terrible situation you went through with your teen even though you were giving your best to use the ACT skills you learned throughout this book. Then complete this exercise:

1. Notice your full experience: "My mind says that I'm..." "My mind says that my teen is..." "I'm feeling..." "My body is having the following sensations..." "I have the urge to..."

2. Name your inner experience. Try to come up with a name for your experience, so you can recognize it if or when it shows up again in a different situation.

3. What's the workability of that inner experience? If you hold on to those thoughts, memories, emotions, sensations, and urges and then act on them, do you move closer toward the parent you want to be? What happens to the relationship with your teen?

4. Defuse from your inner experience if it's not helping you be the parent you want to be.

5. Practice compassionate talk. Can you talk to or relate to yourself the way that a compassionate and caring friend would talk or relate to you in this moment? Write down what your kind friend would tell you at this moment.

Every moment is a new moment to start. Within ACT, you're invited to commit to the process of living your parenting values, not to the process of becoming a perfect parent. Sometimes, despite your best efforts, things are going to be rocky; learning to notice your inner experience, name it, check its workability, defuse from it if it's not helpful, and practice self-compassion is going to make your parenting job a more sustainable one for the better and for the long run.

At the end, every shift you choose to make in your parenting behavior is a new beginning. And every time things go wrong is a new moment to start again.

Starting Again

I was recently talking to my friend Geri about the natural discouragement we all go through when, even after putting our best intention to make a shift in our behavior, things fall apart or our old behaviors quickly fight for survival and take the moment. Geri reminded me of a dharma talk she listened to that highlighted something like this: "Every moment is a new moment, and every moment is a new moment to start." Her words were a reminder of how I can choose to live my personal values from moment to moment; right now I'm reminding you of the same.

Living your parenting values is a choice you face, not only in the middle of a conflict with your teen but on a daily basis and, in reality, from moment to moment. You cannot choose what shows up under your skin; you cannot choose how your teen feels, thinks, or behaves. But you can choose how to respond to that moment. At times, even when you turn on 100 percent willingness, things may have a very different outcome. It's natural; it's part of parenting. It's part of life: not everything goes as we want or hope for it to go. When things go wrong in a moment, it is not an indicator of you being a failure, that nothing is going to change, or that your teen is impossible, even though your mind may come up with thoughts along those lines. When things go wrong, it's an invitation to pause, breathe, acknowledge the struggle of the moment, and check again your parenting values. Checking your values is like checking your true north again.

Finding Your True North Again

Have you ever been lost? Maybe when you were taking a hike in a large park or even when you were driving or visiting a new city? What do we do usually when we are lost? We find a map or, these days, we turn on the GPS in our cars or use the map apps in our cell phones. When things go wrong with your teen, and they simply go south, what's your parenting task? To find your true north again.

How do you find your true north? You ask yourself *What do I want to stand for as parent? What are my values as parent?* Answering these questions will make it easier to figure out your next parenting step. Your parenting values are your true north, and as I often tell my clients, the rest is noise that comes in all forms, such as mind noise, body noise, and even feeling noise. Your parenting values are those parenting qualities that truly matter to you, even if no one knows about them, even if your teen doesn't know about them, even if the outcome is not the ideal one. Checking your parenting values is also not a one-time deal but an ongoing process; the more you check where you're walking as a parent, the more clarity you're going to have about what to do and how to behave, and the stronger sense of fulfillment you're going to have.

Parenting your teen struggling with emotional sensitivity can easily translate into a to-do list of responsibilities, errands, and multiple tasks, and it certainly has all types of moments: good ones, silly ones, tough ones, or absurd ones, to name a few. However, living your parenting life in a way that is driven by your values is ultimately a path that adds meaningful moments to your day. Every one of them, every memory, is a reflection of what matters to you, and every interaction with your teen is touched by meaning; living your parenting values is not pain-free, but it's a way of living life in which you acknowledge that the pain you go through is worthy.

EXERCISE: Finding Your True North

Let's find your true north by mapping your next values-based parenting behavior. Grab your parenting journal, and let's recycle from the situation that didn't go well that you wrote about in the previous exercise. Write down the value that you were pursuing, identify three new goals, potential hooks you may encounter, and ACT helpers you could use in the coming week when taking steps toward that particular parenting value.

When Suzanne did this last exercise, she chose to continue to focus on her parenting value of "caring." The three specific behaviors she came up with were "Ask Catherine to go for a walk with the dog together on Sunday afternoon," "Let Catherine know that I see how frustrating it could be for her when her sister upsets her," and "Ask Catherine if there is anything she could do when she's upset."

Specific hooks for Suzanne were fortune-telling thoughts (*She's not going to listen to me; she may even make fun of me; I can totally see her face saying "This is cheesy, Mom."*), feelings of anxiety, and urges to do nothing at all and let Catherine continue calling her sister names. Suzanne will use a particular ACT helper, including naming her fortune-telling thoughts as "Suzanne the witch." The more you take steps toward your parenting values, the more fulfillment you're going to encounter; a values path is not a pain-free path, but certainly it's a path of meaning.

Last Words

You have reached the end of this book, and by now you have learned all the specialized skills you need to be the best parent possible for your highly sensitive teen.

Your parenting work is not over with this book. The important thing is to keep practicing all the ACT skills you've learned; if you're not quite sure how to implement some of them, then go back to those chapters that cover them in the book, read again, and practice again. You can also choose to go over those skills that are very difficult or that you haven't tried and see what happens if you practice them consistently.

Being an effective parent is accepting that you have challenges in your daily life; the more you allow yourself to choose instead of just react, the more skillful you're going to be when dealing with your teen. The more you make of every moment of challenge a moment to grow, repair, and build a fulfilling relationship with your teen, the better it's going to be. Learning to be the parent you want to be from moment to moment is a parenting life worth living.

Bon voyage to living a parenting life worth living!

Afterword

Parenting an emotionally dysregulated teen is the hardest work in the world. There's a lot of advice available in the media and from mental health professionals for how to do it. Much of the advice is next to useless because it tells you *what* to do—offering skills to better manage your teen's problematic behavior—but not *how* to face the pain when a child reacts aggressively to your new parenting strategies. Techniques, strategies, and skills are not enough. Parents need a way to deal with their own hurt, their own fear, their own discouragement.

That's why acceptance and commitment therapy—the approach offered in Patricia Zurita Ona's excellent book—is your best guide for successfully parenting a dysregulated teen. As you've no doubt discovered reading this book, ACT shows you how to cope with your own emotional struggles while effectively helping your teen to both down-regulate emotions and modulate problematic behavior. The conflict resolution and behavioral management skills are excellent, but, most importantly, they are taught in the context of mindfully observing and accepting your own pain as a parent.

There's another reason the ACT approach promotes more effective parenting for emotionally overwhelmed teens. ACT will help you identify your parenting values—who you want to be to your child—and turn them into committed action. One-size-fits-all parenting protocols don't work very well because they are generic and not tailored to you. This book, by turning your parenting values into specific and profound changes in the relationship to your teen, will reshape your family life. It will make possible a set of new parenting responses that will help your child better regulate and better function at home and in the world.

—Matthew McKay, PhD
 Coauthor of *Thoughts & Feelings* and
 Communication Skills for Teens

Appendix

Some teens suffering with emotion dysregulation problems engage in extreme behaviors involving suicidality, self-injury behaviors, restrictive eating, bingeing, lying, stealing, or experimenting with substances or sexual activity. The purpose of this appendix is to give you a general idea of what to do about these types of problematic situations.

In all these cases, asking for professional guidance is your best course of action. Keep in mind that all these problems are beyond the scope of the ACT parenting tools you have learned in this book; they require help from a mental health provider who works with emotion dysregulation problems. A specialist will come up with recommendations and a plan for you to handle your teen's extreme behaviors; this is not something you can address on your own at home. These types of problematic behaviors require a thorough assessment, close monitoring, and specialized parenting responses.

Wearing Your ACT Glasses When Looking at Extreme Behaviors

Your teen's struggles, whether they involve problematic eating behaviors, alcohol, lying, or suicidal threats, are driven and activated by different sources. However, the uncomfortable, painful emotions your teen is going through and the thoughts or images associated with them are a very common source for all these behaviors. Because your teen suffers with emotional sensitivity, he experiences his emotions at a more intense level than you and I do, as if he had an open wound; he feels anything and everything intensely, and a triggering situation is like salt added to the wound. Therefore, when his emotional switch goes on, he experiences sadness, anxiety, frustration, or another emotion at a maximum level. Then, from that place of emotional sensitivity, he uses a broad range of avoidance strategies, such as thinking about suicide, engaging in self-harm behaviors, overeating or restrictive eating, or smoking marijuana, to name a few emotional avoidance strategies whose purpose is to reduce or turn down the emotional experience. Here is the outcome: your teen's responses work in the short term, but they're not sustainable in the long term, as you may already imagine.

From an ACT point of view, all of your teen's ineffective behaviors are driven by experiential avoidance. Let's briefly go over each one of these problems.

Suicidal and Parasuicidal Behaviors

According to Ross and Heath (2002), in a typical high school in the United States, 14 percent of teens report self-injury at a given time; 12 percent of college students experience self-injurious behaviors. As you can see, parasuicidal behaviors happen often, and many teens struggling with emotional sensitivity struggle with not only parasuicidal but also suicidal behaviors.

Let's start by distinguishing between these two behaviors. *Suicidal behavior* refers specifically to a teen's action with the ultimate goal of ending life and a clear intention to die. *Parasuicidal*, self-injury, or self-harm behaviors, on the other hand, are actions to harm the body in a nonfatal way in response to painful emotional struggles, and they take different forms, such as cutting, burning, picking, or even head banging. Basically, the distinction between these two behaviors is based on the intention or purpose of the behavior on the teen's part.

This distinction is extremely important, since you may be confused at times about your teen's behavior and don't know how to respond to it. Sarah's daughter, Luciana, has been cutting her wrists for the last three months and wears long-sleeve shirts, so no one can see her scars; Sarah only noticed them during breakfast time when Luciana was wearing her PJs. Sarah's mind quickly had the thought *Luciana is killing herself slowly. She just wants to die. Is she trying to punish me? How come I didn't see this before? I should have known how serious her depression was.* Although it's natural that Sarah's mind comes up with all those thoughts, and it may appear that Luciana wants to die, the purpose of cutting is very different from wanting to die.

Most teenagers who engage in self-injury behaviors do so as a way to avoid their psychological struggles. In Luciana's case, she started cutting after learning that her girlfriend's family decided to move to a different state. Upon learning of this, she felt a wave of loneliness and fear, feelings that in her own words "are bigger than her"; she has been cutting whenever she thinks of her friend moving away and imagines what it will be like to spend the weekends alone or have lunch by herself at school.

The above scenario is just one situation that shows why a teen cuts or engages in self-harm behaviors; there could be many other reasons for a teen to cut, such as struggling with school, having fears about being misperceived by friends, memories of traumatic events, feelings of guilt, and so on. Each teen has a different driver of cutting behavior, but here are the two common denominators: your teen is in severe pain and is using an avoidance strategy.

Self-injury behaviors are quick avoidance strategies. It's quite likely that when your teen experiences a very uncomfortable experience, such as a memory, thought, or emotion that is simply intolerable, he doesn't know another way how to handle it—except making the pain go away by using any of these self-harm responses—even though the emotional discomfort he goes through may simply get bigger in the future.

Now if your teen has attempted suicide, clearly with the purpose of ending his life, it's advisable to remove any means that he could use again for attempting suicide until you discuss this with a professional. This means removing any knives, pills, razors, or anything else your teen could use to hurt himself, from his room, the bathrooms, and the household as a whole. As soon as you find a therapist specialized in emotion dysregulation problems, then that provider will offer you specific guidance about how to respond to any other suicide attempt.

If Your Teen Is Making Threats

"If I cannot go out with my boyfriend this weekend, I'll shave my head, and cut my wrists" is an example of a threat. When teens make different types of threats to their parents, it can be very challenging and painful for them. There is no easy response in that moment; if you respond to those threats, you may be augmenting an ineffective behavior, and if you don't respond to those threats, you may still be augmenting other experiences your teen is goes through, such as feelings of loneliness or abandonment. It's a catch-22 for you.

For instance, a client of mine used to make threats to her mother with the purpose of spending time with her. Every time this teen made a threat, her mother sat next to her and comforted her with caring words. Her mother encouraged and praised her and even talked about other matters. As you can see, the mother's behavior was augmenting her daughter's behavior of making threats; this realization only came out after conducting an assessment in a therapy session.

There is no single correct response, because teens make threats with different purposes, intentionally or not. Sometimes your teen makes a threat to get a specific response from you, such as leaving him alone, or when he's trying to avoid doing something or avoid a situation, and without realizing it, your parenting behavior may be reinforcing your teen's behavior. The purpose of your teen's behaviors cannot be assumed as a rule every time he makes a threat, and that's why the guidance of a mental health professional is necessary to give you insight into how to respond.

Problematic Eating Behaviors

Teens suffering with emotion dysregulation problems may also be struggling with restrictive eating, bingeing, purging, anorexia, or bulimia. These behaviors may have started with what seems to be a natural concern of your teen with his body image and shape; however, these behaviors can easily become emotion management strategies and ultimately a disorder that can be fatal for your teen.

Low food consumption and ongoing weight loss as it's seen in anorexia can lead to death.

Teens are usually secretive with these behaviors and their attempts to manage them, because these behaviors are usually associated with high levels of shame. It's a very common reaction for parents I work with to nag their teens about their eating patterns, which is understandable but not helpful.

If you're concerned about your teen's eating patterns, here is what you can do: pay attention to specific cues, such as loss of weight, how often your teen refuses to eat during meal times, fasts, or excessively exercises. Making an appointment with a pediatrician is recommended as a starting point. Get a blood test and a general medical checkup to make sure your teen is safe.

Avoid nagging your teen about his eating behaviors.

Moving forward, you will need the support of a team, including a mental health provider and a nutritionist, so you can receive appropriate coaching from specialists about how to handle these behaviors.

Problematic Substance Abuse

Experimentation with substances is common during adolescence. You may have also heard terms like *substance dependence* or *substance abuse*; regardless of the term, it's important to keep in mind two things. First, experimentation with substances, regardless of the substance, could unfold as an emotion avoidance strategy. For instance, Remy smoked weed as a one-time thing at a party because he was curious about it. Later on, he got fearful about being seen as a fat kid by his classmates, to the point that even wearing baggy clothes to hide his body didn't reduce his fear. He started smoking weed to manage his fears, and he quickly started to rely on it as an emotion avoidance strategy.

Second, using substances as an emotion management strategy could take on a life of its own. Teens struggling with emotional sensitivity feel everything, everywhere, any time, and because their struggle is extremely aversive for them, they will quickly do anything they can to reduce, suppress, or eliminate it. Unfortunately, the combination of drug consumption, withdrawal reactions, and vulnerability to intense emotions could lead them to organize their life around using more and more drugs. In situations like this, a detoxification program may be needed.

Some common interventions involve testing your teen, monitoring the friends he hangs out with, searching his room for substances and removing them, limiting his access to money, or setting a behavioral plan with specific consequences based on the amount and frequency of the substances he uses. The effectiveness of any of these interventions will vary from teen to teen, and therefore it's important to consult with a therapist to come up with a specific plan to address this problem.

The Dangers of Your Friend's Advice

Even though you hear "good advice" from friends or relatives, this is not the time to experiment with your parental responses; without knowing it, you can make an extreme situation worse. Parenting is one thing, but parenting a teen with emotion dysregulation is a different story; everyone knows how to run, but running a marathon requires a different set of skills.

The trouble with listening to the advice of friends or relatives is that they do not always take into consideration the context in which a problematic behavior occurs, the driver of your teen's problematic behavior, or the interaction between you and your teen presents itself. For instance, the advice of "making sure your teen apologizes to you for his behavior" seems very benign and appropriate; however, in context, what if when you get frustrated, you go into dictatorship mode and demand an apology because that was the advice given to you? Would you say that's helpful advice? Does it help your relationship to show your teen that when you're frustrated, you demand a specific response from others? How is your teen learning to handle frustration based on that interaction?

A mental health professional trained in emotion dysregulation problems will come up with specific recommendations that are consistent with the appropriate help your teen needs to receive.

Let's Take a Compassionate Breather...

Up to this point, you have read how ACT understands these complex problematic behaviors for your teen and how important it is to have specialized help from a mental health professional.

It is not easy for you, the parent, or for anyone in your shoes, to handle these types of situations, and naturally you may experience all types of reactions. Even though you have been open to learning all the ACT skills in this book, as well as additional ones, these particular problematic behaviors can be very hard to deal with and are an invitation to pause and check the impact of them on yourself.

Taking a breather and learning to take care of yourself in these moments is very important, since it gives you an opportunity to fuel, recharge, and to start again. Every moment is a new moment to start again.

Acknowledgments

I read a long time ago that it takes a village to make things happen; this book is the result of a village's work!

It wouldn't have been possible to write this book without the learnings from the families, teens, and parents struggling with emotion dysregulation with whom I worked; they taught me the best. Their courage, commitment, and dedication to handle those rocky moments have inspired me over and over again throughout this process.

I'm very grateful to Steven C. Hayes, Kirk Strosahl, and Kelly Wilson, founders of acceptance and commitment therapy (ACT), and the broader ACT community for working hard on helping us make room for the full spectrum of experiences we go through in life and not fragmenting them but instead normalizing, growing, and learning from our pain, sorrow, and struggles. You all have taught me to live a life with purpose!

Special thanks to Ryan Buresh and the editorial department from New Harbinger for their suggestions and comments while I found my way through this project. I would also like to extend special thanks to Catherine Meyers and my dear mentor and life friend, Matt McKay, for facilitating an opportunity for me to write this book. Professor, your teachings are timeless!

Thanks to my colleagues at the East Bay Behavior Therapy Center for all those hallway conversations about different chapters of this book.

I'm also grateful to Andrew Reiner for his kindness and willingness to collaborate on the chapter for fathers or male caregivers. His enthusiasm and concerns about social issues and his eagerness to make a difference are inspiring.

And finally but not least, my sincere appreciation to my village of friends and family: Paolita, Geri, Lucia, Chris, Lynne, Russ, Michael, Maria Delia, Darcy, and Gareth. This work wouldn't exist without your ongoing encouragement, patience, and feedback! Tons of thanks to all of you!

References

Aguirre, B., and G. Galen. 2013. *Mindfulness for Borderline Personality Disorder: Relieve Your Suffering Using the Core Skill of Dialectical Behavior Therapy*. Oakland, CA: New Harbinger Publications.

Centers for Disease Control and Prevention. 2015. "Suicide Facts at a Glance." Web-based Injury Statistics Query and Reporting System (WISQARS). (2013, 2011) National Center for Injury Prevention and Control, CDC (producer). Accessed December 1, 2016. Available from http://www.cdc.gov/injury/wisqars/index.html.

Ciarrochi, J., A. Bailey, and R. Harris. 2014. *The Weight Escape: How to Stop Dieting and Start Living*. Boulder, CO: Shambhala Publications.

Eifert, G. H., M. McKay, and J. P. Forsyth. 2006. *ACT on Life Not on Anger: The New Acceptance and Commitment Therapy Guide to Problem Anger*. Oakland, CA: New Harbinger Publications.

Gilbert, P. 2010. *The Compassionate Mind: A New Approach to Life's Challenges*. Oakland, CA: New Harbinger Publications.

Goleman, D. 1995. *Emotional Intelligence: Why It Can Matter More Than IQ*. New York: Bantam Books.

Gottman, J., and N. Silver. 1999. *The Seven Principles for Making Marriage Work*. New York: Harmony Books.

Harris, R. 2009. *ACT Made Simple*. Oakland, CA: New Harbinger Publications.

Hayes, S. C. 2016. "State of the ACT Evidence." Association for Contextual Behavioral Science. Accessed December 1. https://contextual science.org/state_of_the_act_evidence.

Hayes, S. C., D. Barnes-Holmes, and B. Roche, eds. 2001. *Relational Frame Theory: A Post-Skinnerian Account of Human Language and Cognition*. New York: Plenum Press.

Hayes, S. C., K. D. Strosahl, and K. G. Wilson. 1999. *Acceptance and Commitment Therapy: An Experiential Approach to Behavior Change*. New York: Guilford Press.

———. 2012. *Acceptance and Commitment Therapy: The Process and Practice of Mindful Change*. 2nd ed. New York: Guilford Press.

Hayes, S. C., K. D. Strosahl, K. G. Wilson, R. T. Bissett, J. Pistorello, D. Toarmino, M. Polusny, T. A. Dykstra, S. V. Batten, J. Bergan, S. H. Stewart, M. J. Zvolensky, G. H. Eifert, F. W. Bond, J. P. Forsyth, M. Karekla, and S. M. McCurry. 2004. "Measuring Experiential Avoidance: A Preliminary Test of a Working Model." *The Psychological Record* 54 (4): 553–78.

Kabat-Zinn, Jon. 1990. *Full Catastrophe Living: Using the Wisdom of Your Body and Mind to Face Stress, Pain, and Illness.* New York: Delacorte Press.

———. 2005. Wherever You Go, There You Are. 10th ed. New York: Hachette Books.

Mansfield, A. K., M. Addis, and J. R. Mahalik. 2003. "'Why Won't He Go to the Doctor?': The Psychology of Men's Help Seeking." *International Journal of Men's Health.* 2 (2): 93–109.

McKay, M., M. Davis, and P. Fanning. 2009. *Messages: The Communication Skills Book.* 3rd ed. Oakland, CA: New Harbinger Publications.

Patterson, G., and M. Forgatch 2005. *Parents and Adolescents Living Together Part 1: The Basics.* 2nd ed. Champaign, IL: Research Press.

Ross, S., and N. L. Heath. 2002. "A Study of the Frequency of Self-Mutilation in a Community Sample of Adolescents." *Journal of Youth and Adolescence* 31 (1): 67–77.

Siegel, D. J. 1999. *The Developing Mind: Toward a Neurobiology of Interpersonal Experience.* New York: Guilford Press.

Strosahl, K., P. Robinson, and T. Gustavsson. 2012. *Brief Interventions for Radical Change: Principles and Practice of Focused Acceptance and Commitment Therapy.* Oakland, CA: New Harbinger Publications.

Tavris, C. 1989. *Anger: The Misunderstood Emotion.* Rev. ed. New York: Simon and Schuster.

Thompson, M. 2011. "Why Do So Many Boys Not Care About School?" *PBS Parents.* February 6. http://www.pbs.org/parents/experts/archive /2011/01/why-so-many-boys-dont-care-abo.html.

Tirch, D., B. Schoendorff, and L. R. Silberstein. 2014. *The ACT Practitioner's Guide to the Science of Compassion: Tools for Fostering Psychological Flexibility.* Oakland, CA: New Harbinger Publications.

Wilson, K. 2008. *Mindfulness for Two: An Acceptance and Commitment Therapy Approach to Mindfulness in Psychotherapy.* Oakland, CA: New Harbinger Publications.

Wilson, K., and T. Dufrene. 2010. *Things Might Go Terribly, Horribly Wrong: A Guide to Life Liberated from Anxiety.* Oakland, CA: New Harbinger Publications.

Patricia E. Zurita Ona, PsyD, is director of the East Bay Behavior Therapy Center and adjunct professor at the Wright Institute. Her clinical work started first as school psychologist, and then as a clinical psychologist. She has significant experience working with children, adolescents, and adults with mood, anxiety, and body-image concerns; particular areas of expertise are obsessive-compulsive disorder (OCD) and post-traumatic stress disorder (PTSD). Zurita Ona also provides specialized services for individuals struggling with emotional dysregulation problems, such as borderline personality disorder (BPD), with or without self-harm and suicidal behaviors. She is coauthor of *Mind and Emotions*, a universal protocol for emotional disorders that has received a "Self-Help Seal of Merit" from the Association for Behavioral and Cognitive Therapies (ABCT).

Foreword writer **Kirk D. Strosahl, PhD**, is cofounder of acceptance and commitment therapy (ACT), a cognitive behavioral approach that has gained widespread adoption in the mental health and substance-abuse communities. He is coauthor of *Brief Interventions for Radical Change* and *In This Moment*. Strosahl provides training and consultation services for Mountainview Consulting Group, Inc. He is a pioneer in the movement to bring behavioral health services into primary care. He resides in Portland, OR.

Afterword writer **Matthew McKay, PhD**, is a professor at the Wright Institute in Berkeley, CA. He has authored and coauthored numerous books, including *The Relaxation and Stress Reduction Workbook*, *Self-Esteem*, *Thoughts and Feelings*, *When Anger Hurts*, and *ACT on Life Not on Anger*. McKay received his PhD in clinical psychology from the California School of Professional Psychology, and specializes in the cognitive behavioral treatment of anxiety and depression. He lives and works in the greater San Francisco Bay Area.

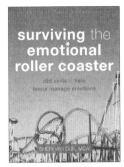

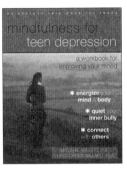